To my mother,
a true compass, in the kitchen and elsewhere.
The sound of your rings as you're dusting a cake
pan with flour still accompanies me to this day.

To my grandmother,
who was a brilliant storyteller for everything,
but especially when it came to food and
tales of meals past. Thank you for teaching
me to be particular about everything.

A SPOONFUL

Mediterranean Cookbook
for All Seasons

Pauline Chardin

OF SUN

gestalten

NOTES FROM MY LAND
OF PLENTY

A couple of years ago, I moved from Paris to a modern house in a village in Provence. I had always been passionate about food, but freed from the culinary distractions of big-city living, I felt my cooking was taking root for the first time. Before settling here, I had traveled the world, unknowingly collecting the intuitions that would turn this new house into a home, this new kitchen into my own.

I wasn't born in this corner of Provence, yet moving here felt like a return to my origins and the fulfilling of an old dream, one that had preceded me. I had spent many summer holidays around here and grew up listening to the tales of my parents, whose minds always seemed to wander back to this promised land. Our family photo albums are filled with holiday pictures of me gorging on pears half the size of my head, sweet juice rolling down my blissed-out face. We used to visit friends of my family who happened to be fruit producers. I remember the old farm as a southern wonderland, with mountains of peach crates stacked in the courtyard, icy glasses of almond syrup, and piles of cantaloupes on the lunch table.

When the desire to leave the city became insistent, it was the obvious choice to build here, in the southern part of the Drôme region. It is a place that manages to be both intense and mellow, enchanting and rough, one that seems to have inspired the expression "land of plenty." Eating local is almost too easy here and, contrary to when I lived in Paris, it makes absolute sense. Good local products abound and the idea of buying something that doesn't grow here quickly felt incongruous. Don't misread me—the land is generous but still maintains a tension between scarcity and abundance, one I came to realize makes everything all the more precious. Not everything is available, and certainly not all the time, but I've come to appreciate these little quirks. They make me feel like I live in a very specific place instead of numbing myself with the illusion that you can have anything if you pay the price.

As I settled in here, it surprised me how taken I was with observing the cyclical changes in nature, and syncing myself and my cooking with them brought me no small dose of happiness. Following these ever-renewing cycles solves a large part of the dilemma of craving newness in your meals. You come to realize that one ingredient or recipe has its often-short moment; it is available, and therefore feels right, at a particular time before disappearing for months. During the time it's gone, I can either crave it or forget it altogether, but in both cases, meeting again is a renaissance of sorts. I finally understood that the food fatigue I used to feel while living in Paris stemmed from constant access to everything. It dulled my senses and made food an emotionless convenience. In Provence, I came to love the idea of seizing the moment with ingredients. It's a way of putting the focus back on the product; cooking the right thing at the right time is a reward in itself.

In that spirit, you will see that the book is arranged in a seasonal way. I'm happy to confirm that the cliché of Provence being a place of everlasting sunshine feels pretty true when you've spent most of your life in a much darker, northern climate. I often think that the abundance and quality of the light here are the things I cherish most. Still, each moment of the year has its own, sometimes very fleeting, taste. That's why, beyond the four traditional seasons, I also wanted to include chapters dedicated to the half seasons. I find these in-betweens very inspiring—they're much-needed transitions that help me to renounce what's ending while offering an enticing taste of the season approaching. They are emotional times in which melancholy and excitement co-exist, and for me all these rich feelings show in the food I cook and eat.

Relocating myself to Provence deepened an already strong connection to the Mediterranean and its cooking traditions. Having traveled to Italy, Greece, Spain, Lebanon, and North Africa, I could grasp the many differences but, more importantly, I could see the common ground and it made sense to be inspired by all these parts of the Mediterranean to cook my everyday meals. I had always been drawn toward that school of cooking, but seeing the big jars of olive oil in my cellar and the crates of tomatoes on my porch there was no doubt in my mind I was finally home.

The recipes that follow are built around vegetables and fruit. For me, leaning heavily toward a vegetarian diet is above all motivated by taste. Still, I might not be so passionate if it didn't also have the health benefit of making me feel good. A long time ago now, I discovered that a plant-driven diet with smaller portions was a great fit for a modern life where work is done mostly indoors. This might feel a bit austere to some, but I'm counting on this book to convince you that it isn't. I see myself as much a creature of pleasure as one of reason and that fine balance probably shows in what I cook.

Between the recipes you'll find pages that retrace some of the inspirations and context behind my cooking. I hope they will help paint a larger picture, shine a light on the origins of some passions of mine, and get you into the mindset of one moment or place. I was eager to show how the things I've seen and experienced have influenced my home-cooking and how traditional dishes can find their way into modern life. Writing this book, I realized how much I associate food with memories and taste with aesthetic sensations. I think of food the way I think of drawing or painting: as a daily creative endeavor, no matter how mundane it might seem.

That may be in part because I was raised in a family in which food is an all-time preoccupation and a beloved topic of conversation. A good meal will just as surely lift my mood as a bad one will ruin it. This is a sensitive matter to me, and yet I believe in approaching it in an instinctive and easygoing way. The cooking that concerns me most, and which this book is about, is the cooking that happens every day. Mine is mostly the product of an impatient mind that won't compromise on eating well. I don't like to plan ahead, I keep measuring to a minimum, and I favor versatile ideas that will adapt to whatever's in season. Don't get me wrong; I absolutely believe terrific cooking comes from patience. But I also believe you should find a cooking style that fits your character and work from there. In cooking, as in life, you have to pick your battles. Your time and energy are limited. Right now, I'm not that person who soaks chickpeas overnight. But I can be the one who makes homemade ravioli because that's satisfying to me. Don't let cookbooks shame you into doing something you resent!

Cooking should not be a hassle, and if you follow your heart, it never is.

In my mind, what you choose to eat should be the product of your mood at a particular moment. I'd rather spend time wondering what I really crave instead of mindlessly cooking with whatever is in my fridge. I might choose to make the same dish extra spicy one day or not at all a few months later. The only right choice is the one that fits the moment. These minor tweaks, whether coming from a whim or simply a lack of resources, make recipes more personal and might lead to small discoveries that will stay with you for years.

Finally, I want to give you credit for picking up this book and maybe trying to cook from it. It takes a bit of courage to try anything new, in a kitchen no less than anywhere else. Learning new things is something us adults don't do all that often and I'm hoping I'll make it worth your while.

Pauline Chardin

EARLY SPRING

028

054

LATE SPRING

EARLY SUMMER

084

112

LATE SUMMER

EARLY FALL  140

168 LATE FALL

EARLY WINTER  196

224 LATE WINTER

PANTRY
ESSENTIALS

With all the conveniences available in a big city or in the comfort of a well-known kitchen, it's easy to lose sight of the basis of your cooking: finding the shortest way to a satisfying and healthy meal. Cooking abroad, sometimes with the bare minimum, and cooking in our new countryside kitchen, helped shed light on what I find essential. I think there is more romance in making meals from a few good staples than from an overstocked pantry. Something about aiming for survival and ending up with pleasure really resonates with me.

FRESH VEGETABLES
AND FRUIT

A meal without fresh produce feels like a sorry prospect to me. To cook and season them, chances are I will reach out for the olive oil jar. We drink more olive oil than wine in our house and a vast majority of what I cook relies on it. I only use the extra-virgin kind and keep two bottles on hand—one for cooking, and a pricier one to be consumed raw. Excellent olive oil makes everything better—find out which kind you prefer and say goodbye to complicated dressings. If I took my own advice, which I often do, I would season any salad with just olive oil, fleur de sel, and freshly ground black pepper. Garlic—the purple kind—would also be at the top of my list. I tend to use it raw when it's young, in the spring and summer, and cook it for a deeper taste during the fall and winter. I'm also prompt to grate it so its flavor can be diffused quickly.

DAIRY
PRODUCTS

While I eat cheese in moderate quantities, there is always a small sample of them in the fridge. I like the idea of incorporating cheese in recipes, versus the classic French idea of having all the cheeses on a board in the middle of the meal. I always have on hand Parmigiano-Reggiano and brousse, a fresh cheese from Provence made from the whey of either cow, ewe, or goat's milk. My other dairy of choice is Greek yogurt, whose sourness works well in savory recipes. A dollop on top of spicy dishes is a good way to balance flavors and its thick texture makes it a great substitute for heavy cream.

MEAT AND
EGGS

Meat as a dish in itself has disappeared from my diet a long time ago. Instead, every now and then, I use meat products as seasoning. A bit of 'nduja, a few cuts of coppa, help add that otherwise hard-to-get smoky flavor. This requires very small quantities and feels like a responsible way to use it. Dispensing with meat has probably made a bigger place for eggs in my diet. In addition to eating them fried all year round with seasonal vegetables, I poach them on rice and fold them in cereal patties, pies, and pastries.

PASTA AND GRAINS

What would life be without pasta and rice? The former made from semola di grano duro and bronze-cut, the latter open to variety: basmati, Thai, red, black, whole, Japanese … but also from Camargue, not far from where we live. In an attempt to foster grain diversity, I also welcome polenta, millet, einkorn, or quinoa in my kitchen.

FLOUR AND SUGAR

I tell myself I could live on fruit, but still, life would be a bit sad without cakes and pastries. Which brings us to the subject of sugar. In my pantry it's of the unrefined kind for almost every use and it shares the sweetening duties with honey, agave, date, and maple syrup.

I was raised to make dough from scratch, and this is much more exciting with a sample of different flours on hand—it also helps me break away from using only regular wheat. In addition to my base of all-purpose flour (French T65) I always have einkorn, rice, Manitoba, and semola on hand. Beyond these, I welcome a rotation of spelt, chestnut, chickpea, blue corn, and rye.

NUTS, SPICES, AND HERBS

Finally, there are the not-so-little things that might not feed you but that will enrich your meals greatly. On my shelves, nuts and seeds abound, both for snacking and cooking purposes. I also keep a tidy spice stash that includes different chilies, cumin, cinnamon, coriander, and turmeric. And, last but not least, the herbs. If they were more readily accessible, I would use mountains of fresh aromatics. The image of Middle Eastern markets piled with cheap herbs remains a fantasy to this day. The reality is slightly more reasonable but allows for some variety between what can be bought and grown in our garden. One of the benefits of growing your own herbs is that you get to use the flowers in your cooking. Look out for fragrant coriander, sage, and spring onion flowers, which have a way of making a plate feel special. Fresh herbs are a luxury, but the more reliable dried ones also play a significant role in my kitchen. Oregano, thyme, and rosemary get more fragrant once they're dried. Picked in the wild or from my garden, they will be useful all year round but are especially precious in the winter to perfume soups, sauces, and oils.

A
KITCHEN
INVENTORY

I'm writing "inventory" but I'm starting to think this looks more like a portrait. I like that this personal and by no means "perfect" array reveals the bargains we make between functionality and sentiments. Surely both these things have a big place in my kitchen and it shows in the objects that fill it.

I like the idea that cooking should not require too much fancy gear. Simple, efficient and good looking tools are the bulk of what fill my kitchen drawers. I'm wary of any big piece of machinery that might clutter my counter or cupboards, but will happily collect handmade wooden spatulas and treasure used up items inherited from my mother or grand-mother's kitchens. In the same spirit, I'm always open to the low investment, slightly quirky tools that stem from tradition. Having a wooden gnocchi board sounds more useful to me than a multifunction mixer.

Looking at the items on these pages, bear in mind that I mostly ever cook for a few people, and my tools reflect that. I don't need to do things in huge quantities, instead I need efficient solutions for 2–4 people, 8 at the most. This remains a work in progress and I'm always on the hunt for that surprisingly elegant iteration of that usually ugly item, for the life-changing tool you didn't know existed or for yet another set of hand-carved salad servers.

PREPPING

1 A set of graters, fine for ginger and hard cheese, medium for vegetables.

2 A citrus squeezer, to avoid getting seeds in your dish.

3 A set of mixing bowls—two is the minimum.

4 A bamboo grater brush, for ginger or anything that sticks.

5 An adjustable mandoline, an excellent ally for swift prep.

6 A set of strainers of different sizes, to rinse cereals, drain pasta, and wash produce.

7 Kitchen scissors, big enough to spot right away.

8 Rolling pins: a big one for pies, a small one for flatbreads.

9 A silicon spatula, to get all the batter in a few swoops.

10 A wooden tea spoon, also very handy for coarse salt.

11 A set of whisks, small and medium.

12 A mushroom brush—much better than water.

13 An ever-expanding collection of mortars, in wood, brass, or stone, for sauces and spices.

14 A Chinese mooncake wooden mold, to hold eggs while I bake.

15 A duo of vintage stoneware jugs with corks, for olive oil.

16 A hand blender, for soups and ice cream.

17 A solid bread knife, because I like slim slices.

18 A duo of Japanese knives: office (5 in./12 cm) and santoku (7 in./17 cm).

19 A peeler, also handy to cut fine strips.

20 A wooden gnocchi board, a humble eccentricity.

21 A garlic crusher, in metal to weather daily use.

22 An efficient salad dryer. I find washing salad tedious; this makes it slightly better.

23 An electronic scale, a sometimes-necessary evil.

24 A heavy-duty pepper grinder, to survive intensive use.

25 A hand electric mixer, for egg whites and chantilly.

26 A small mixer, for nuts, parmigiano, and quick sauces.

27 Cutting boards, to prep and serve. Olive-tree wood and fragrant hinoki are favorites.

COOKING AND SERVING

1   A straw plate cover, to keep flies at bay in style.

2   A bamboo steamer basket: so simple yet so efficient.

3   One large and one tiny kitchen mitt, the latter from Japan.

4   Bamboo and metal tongs, to flip and catch.

5   A foldable pizza peel—but I could be convinced to get a wooden one and hang it with pride.

6   Wooden spreader knives, somewhere between primitive and refined.

7   A brass skimming ladle, to fish poached eggs and ravioli.

8   Wooden salad servers, like heirlooms.

9   A flat pan, a frying pan, and a grill pan in non-stick stone.

10 A sample of beautiful trivets, because one can never have enough.

11 A big pasta pot, so indispensable I forgive its size.

12 A stoneware dish, for gratins and lasagna.

13 A collection of bread and fruit baskets that look as good empty as they do filled.

14 Spaghetti tongs, to avoid making a mess.

15 Two metal spatulas—the shorter one, from French brand Nogent, is a trusty ally for handling delicate foods.

16 A collection of wooden spatulas, spoons, and pie servers made by various craftspeople.

17 A set of lids—I hate a pan without a matching one.

18 A glass cloche, to pretend I live in a nice coffee shop.

19 A wooden salt cellar and its brass spoon, for fleur de sel. Travels between the kitchen and the table.

20 Removable-bottom pie pans, including a 7 in. (17 cm)-wide one for flans and very small gatherings.

21 A smooth horn rice spoon, to cajole fragile grains.

22 Tartelette pans, to triumph over the crumbliest crusts.

23 Saucepans: one big, one small.

24 A pizza stone, for crispy dough.

25 Round, square, and long cake pans in different sizes.

26 A Le Creuset cocotte from the '70s, inherited from my mother.

27 An aluminum baking tray, lighter and easier to clean than steel.

EARLY

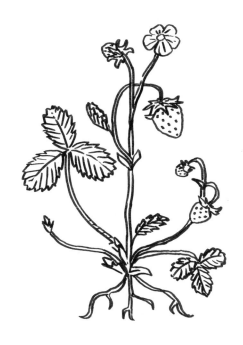

SPRING

Watching the first days of spring unfurl is a very emotional, fragile time. As I look for every new sign in breathless anticipation, careful not to pronounce the arrival of spring too early, I start to remember the sweetness of the season to come, almost within my grasp.

This is the moment when I cut all the dry flowers in the garden, whose silhouettes kept the memory of spring alive all winter long. That simple task feels like an act of faith: I let go of the past year and trust that new leaves will come soon. My very human impatience is tempered by a deep respect for the terrific forces at work in a single sprout. It's rebirth after all, and it can't be rushed.

The weather itself echoes the intensity of the awakening, drenching the garrigue in violent showers before shining a blinding light on what looks like a new world, greens brighter and tiny blooms scintillating with raindrops. In the kitchen, every new product is a cause for celebration. Here come the asparagus, the wild garlic, the strawberries! They bring with them a renewed energy, and the magic of new beginnings seems to wash over the remaining winter products and pantry staples. For an instant, the old and new live together, renegotiating the balance between comfort and novelty at every meal.

FARINATA
WITH RUCOLA SALAD

INGREDIENTS

FOR THE FARINATA

7 oz. (200 g) chickpea
    flour
2½ cups (600 ml) water
1 tsp. fine salt
rosemary and
    savory sprigs
    (optional)
7 tbsp. olive oil
pepper

FOR THE SALAD

2 handfuls rucola
2 tbsp. capers
2 tbsp. toasted pine
    nuts
2¾ oz. (75 g) torn
    mozzarella di bufala
    (optional)
1 tbsp. lemon juice
a splash of olive oil

When I travel, I often fall in love with the simplest dish or ingredients. I obsess over them, tweak itineraries to eat them one more time, and very soon I am planning fantasy trips in my head with the sole purpose of eating that particular thing again. In that spirit, I often muse about driving to Genoa to order farinata at Sà Pesta trattoria, because what are five hours of driving if I get to eat it again?
Farinata is a crispy chickpea galette from Liguria. Originally a street-food staple, it is best eaten very hot with loads of cracked pepper. I found that you can still make a good version at home if Genoa is too far a drive for dinner.

Put the chickpea flour in a mixing bowl. This particular kind of flour tends to make clumps, so use a fork to get it as smooth as you can. Make a well in the center of the flou and add the water in three additions, whisking thoroughly each time. You will obtain a homogenous, very liquid batter. Cover and leave it to rest at room temperature for 4–8 hours.

When ready to cook, pre-heat your oven at 600 °F (300 °C).

Meanwhile, skim off the foam on the batter if any has formed. Add the salt, whisk to make it smooth and transfer to an oiled 14 × 12 in. (36 × 30 cm) non-stick oven dish. It should be no thicker than ½ in. (1 cm).

Top with the herb sprigs, if using. With a spoon, drizzle the olive oil on the surface, without mixing it. Oil bubbles should form on the surface. Cook in the oven for around 15 minutes, until it becomes brown or even dark brown on the edges.

Put the salad ingredients in a mixing bowl. Wait until the last minute to mix.

When ready to serve, carefully get the farinata out of the oven, crack a generous amount of pepper on top, cut it into quarters and use a spatula to transfer to plates. Top with the rucola salad and eat while it's hot.

For the farinata, the hotter the oven, the better. If your oven doesn't go up to 600 °F (300 °C), try cooking at a lower temperature and finishing it with a few minutes of grill.

I often serve this as a light meal, eating only half of the farinata. The remaining part tastes great re-fried with a bit of olive oil in a pan.

You can skip the mozzarella in the salad but I love the freshness it brings.

Look for good-quality capers preserved in olive oil. If you don't have them on hand, try replacing them with good olives or sun-dried tomatoes.

SERVES 2 AS A MAIN
COOKING TIME 15 MINUTES
RESTING TIME 4–8 HOURS

WILD GARLIC PESTO PASTA
WITH ASPARAGUS

INGREDIENTS

FOR THE PASTA

10 green asparagus
8¾ oz. (250 g) long
    pasta or trofie
2 tbsp. olive oil
salt, pepper

FOR THE PESTO

1¾ oz. (50 g) pine nuts
1¾ oz. (50 g) Parmigiano-
    Reggiano, roughly
    cut in small chunks
a small handful
    of wild garlic
a splash of olive oil

Wild garlic grows in humid woodlands at the beginning of spring. It has a green garlic taste and plays the role of garlic in my kitchen before the new ones arrive on market stalls a few weeks later. It is one of the very welcome signs of early spring, and it's hard not to be amazed at nature producing tender, fragrant leaves again. At a time when fresh ingredients are a bit scarce, I feel grateful that nature goes to the trouble of offering a versatile leaf that manages to replace two of the ingredients of classic pesto: basil and garlic.

When I'm very hungry, it seems like the only thing my mind can conjure as a solution is a plate of pasta. Taking into account the very limited energy and patience I have when starving, I need the kind of recipe that can be put together in the time it takes for pasta to cook. This is the green, springy answer to that emergency situation.

Put salted water to boil for the pasta.

Prepare the asparagus, discarding the tough ends and cutting them into 2 in. (5 cm) chunks before slicing them lengthwise in barely ½ in. (1 cm) thick bands.

Toast the pine nuts in a hot pan. Don't let them out of your sight, these burn easily. As soon as they get brown, transfer them to the bowl of your food processor.

Put the pasta in the boiling water. With this kind of pasta you have around 10 minutes before it's ready, which should be enough to make your pesto and cook the asparagus.

Add the rest of the pesto ingredients to your food processor and start blitzing. Add olive oil as needed until you have a spreadable paste.

Heat 2 tablespoons of olive oil on medium-high heat in a non-stick pan and put in your asparagus with a bit of salt and pepper. Mix so the oil coats them. Cover and leave to cook for around 4 minutes. They should brown slightly and not turn completely soft.

Before draining the pasta, gather the equivalent of a glass of pasta cooking water. Drain the pasta and while it sits in the strainer, transfer the pesto to the pasta pot. Add a bit of cooking water, just enough (around 3½ tbsp.) to make the pesto looser and lighter. Add the drained pasta and stir well on medium heat for a couple of minutes, allowing the sauce to coat the pasta.

Transfer to your serving plates and top with the asparagus.

7 oz. (200 g) of pasta would probably be a more reasonable amount for pasta for two people, but I have trouble enforcing that number at home!

Spaghetti, linguine or tagliatelle would all work well here, but if you can find trofie, the traditional pasta shape from Liguria, it has been designed to work with pesto.

Wild garlic can either be foraged or bought from small sellers. If the season has passed, you can replace it with a mix of basil and spinach sprouts, and add a garlic clove to the mix.

You can double pesto quantities and keep it for salad dressings or sandwiches.

GARDEN POTATOES WITH
GREENS AND FRESH FLOWERS

INGREDIENTS

4 medium-sized firm
   yet tender potatoes,
   peeled and cut into
   quarters
2 tbsp. sunflower seeds
1 tbsp. fennel seeds
a few fresh tarragon
   sprigs, roughly
   chopped
a few wild fennel
   greens sprigs,
   roughly chopped
a few basil leaves,
   roughly chopped
1 very small garlic clove,
   crushed
5 tbsp. olive oil
10½ oz. (300 g) of a
   mix of spring greens
   (snow peas, aspara-
   gus, peas, fava beans),
   ready to be steamed
2 tbsp. taggiasche
   olives
salt, pepper
aromatic flowers (thyme,
   sage, rosemary...)
2 generous tbsp.
   fresh cheese such
   as brousse or ricotta
   (optional)

I guess the city version of me didn't care much for potatoes as soon as winter was over. Living in the countryside made me remember that they can be as springy or summery as you'd like them to be.
This is a dish for the early days of spring, when the first bright greens arrive and the first flowers bloom. I like that it's comforting and vibrant at the same time. Adding flowers to the dish really helps to make it special. For a long time I believed edible flowers were mysterious little things you'd buy for a fortune in a fancy grocery store. As it turns out, your aromatic plants are willing to give you flavorful flowers for free. Thyme, rosemary, mint or, in this recipe, sage flowers are great additions to spring dishes.

Arrange the potatoes in a single layer in the base of a steaming basket and steam them.

Meanwhile, toast the sunflower and fennel seeds in a pan. Remove when the seeds turn golden and fragrant, and transfer to a bowl to cool.

Put the chopped herbs with your crushed garlic and olive oil in a mixing bowl big enough to hold all the ingredients.

When the potatoes are almost done, put the other greens to steam on top of them. If you're using snow peas, wait until the last moment as they're very fast to cook.

Transfer the steamed vegetables to the mixing bowl, add the olives and seeds and mix thoroughly. Add salt and pepper to taste.

Don't worry about serving it right away. It's actually nicer when not too hot. When you're ready, divide into bowls, add the flowers and fresh cheese, if using. Feel free to drizzle with more olive oil.

Taggiasche olives, from which the delicious Ligurian oil is often made, are favorites of mine.

You don't necessarily have to mix several greens for this recipe to work. If you only have peas for instance, it will still be great.

SERVES 2 AS A LIGHT MEAL
COOKING TIME 15 MINUTES

1

GORGED WITH SPRING RAINS, THE ROCKY
LANDSCAPE OF THE GARRIGUE CHANGES
SEEMINGLY OVERNIGHT. THE TOUGHEST PLANTS
EXPLODE IN A MYRIAD OF TINY FLOWERS
AND SPROUTS THAT WILL SURELY TRANSFORM
ANY PLATE INTO A CELEBRATION.

1   Baby radish, wild fennel, tarragon, and aphyllanthes salad.

2   It's uncanny to see this landscape of rocks and thorns dressed in tender greens and pinks.

ASPARAGUS, MUSHROOM, AND TAHINI SALAD

INGREDIENTS

FOR THE SALAD

3 medium-sized,
   very fresh button
   mushrooms,
   thinly sliced
2 handfuls mesclun
2 tbsp. olive oil
1 tbsp. fennel seeds
1 tbsp. coriander seeds
10 green asparagus,
   cut lengthwise in
   3 in. (7 cm) pieces
salt, pepper
2 tbsp. brousse
   or ricotta cheese
1 tbsp. Kasha

flatbread or einkorn
   bread, to serve

FOR THE DRESSING

3 tbsp. olive oil
1 rounded tsp. whole
   tahini
1 tbsp. lemon juice
salt, pepper

Asparagus grows remarkably well in the sandy soil where we live and its arrival is the first notable sign of spring, vegetable-wise. For a few weeks it monopolizes the market stalls and are my go-to greens. They disappear as other vegetables arrive, just when you start to run out of ideas for how to eat them. It's a short and intense season and I always feel a tiny bit melancholic when I'm told I'm buying the last ones: did I make the most of them?

This hybrid between a salad and sautéed vegetables is perfect for the early days of spring, when you want something greener but still crave a bit of comfort in the still-fresh evenings.

Assemble the dressing ingredients in a salad bowl. Add the sliced mushrooms and the mesclun but wait until you serve to mix gently.

Heat the olive oil on medium heat in a non-stick pan. Add the fennel and coriander seeds and the asparagus a minute later. Season with salt and pepper to taste. Cover and let cook until some of the asparagus have gained some color but retain a slight bite. You do not want them to turn too soft.

Arrange the salad and mushrooms on serving plates, top with the cooked asparagus and a tablespoon of brousse per plate.

Use the asparagus pan to toast the kasha seeds for a couple minutes before adding them to each plate. Serve with flatbread or a slice of einkorn bread.

To taste good raw, mushrooms need to be extra fresh and firm—look underneath the caps to see if they are still white.

Kasha is roasted buckwheat. It can be boiled like a cereal but I prefer to use it as a crunchy seed to top salads or even desserts.

Try having asparagus on sourdough bread with mozzarella or just with a fried egg and parmigiano.

Whole tahini, sometimes sold just as whole sesame paste, tastes richer and has long replaced the classic variety in my kitchen.

SERVES 2 AS A LIGHT MEAL
COOKING TIME 5–10 MINUTES

LEEK AND
'NDUJA DUMPLINGS

INGREDIENTS

FOR THE FILLING

3 tbsp. sesame oil
1 garlic clove, crushed
¾ in. (2 cm) fresh
    ginger, grated
1 tbsp. 'nduja
3 oz. (80 g) fennel,
    finely chopped
5½ oz. (160 g) leeks, cut
    into ½ in. (1 cm) slices
1 tbsp. unrefined sugar
1 tbsp. soy sauce
1 spring onion, finely
    chopped

FOR THE WRAPPERS

4½ oz. (125 g) all-purpose
    flour
½ tsp. fine salt
⅓ cup (75 ml) hot water
a handful of corn starch
4 tbsp. sesame oil

FOR THE SAUCE

3 tbsp. soy sauce
1 tbsp. rice vinegar
1 tbsp. sesame oil

TOPPINGS

a few coriander sprigs
1 spring onion,
    finely chopped

It's hard to get excited again about leeks when you've spent all winter with them, but add a bit of spice and the freshness of brand new spring onions and they can finish the season in style.
For all my talk of being a slightly impatient cook, I'm also one with a passion for handcrafting tiny portions of food. Gnocchi, ravioli, briwats, dumplings… I find making all of these very satisfying and I'm forever proud that I can make from scratch things that seemed either too mysterious or too laborious before.

Start by making the filling. Heat the sesame oil in a non-stick pan. Add the garlic, ginger, and 'nduja. Mix well and leave to cook for a couple of minutes. Add the fennel and leeks, mix to coat, add the sugar and soy sauce and mix again. Cover and leave to cook on medium-high heat for 12–15 minutes, until soft and slightly caramelized. Transfer to a bowl so it cools down.

Prepare the dough for the wrappers. In a bowl, mix the flour with the salt, make a well and add the hot water. Mix roughly with a fork before using your hands. Knead for 5–10 minutes, until smooth and not sticky. Leave to rest, covered, for at least 30 minutes. In a small bowl, mix the sauce ingredients and leave aside to rest.

Once the dough has rested, poke a hole in the middle with your thumb (like a donut), stretch it carefully and cut it in one place with a knife so you have a long tube. Cut the dough into 12 equal parts (roughly ½ oz. (17 g) per portion). Put a handful of corn starch on your kitchen counter (or wooden board) and with a small rolling pin, start rolling each portion into a 4 in. (10 cm)-wide circle. Layer them into a pile, dusting them with starch so they don't stick to each other.

Add the chopped spring onion to your cooked filling, and mix.

To make the dumplings, have a small bowl of water and a large platter next to your work station. Holding the dough circle in your hand, place a teaspoon of filling in the middle. With the tip of your finger, moisten the lower border of the circle. Quickly fold the circle on itself, sealing the top middle point, before folding one side over the other. I like to make at least 4 pleats on each side. Put the finished dumplings on a platter as you go.

Heat 4 tablespoons of sesame oil in a large non-stick pan. Carefully but quickly put your dumplings to cook side by side. Leave to cook on high heat for 2 minutes before adding water to the pan (up to ¼ of the dumplings' height). Cover and leave to cook for 5 minutes, until all water has evaporated and the dough looks lighter and softer. Remove the lid and cook for 2 more minutes to get them extra crispy on the bottom.

Divide them between two plates, pour sauce in each individual saucer and top with the coriander sprigs and chopped spring onion.

'Nduja is a spicy pork sausage from Calabria. Its soft, spreadable texture makes it a great condiment. It is often sold in small jars and will give some fiery depth to everything it touches. Add a spoonful to a regular tomato sauce and you're in for a spicy treat.

If you want to keep it vegetarian, try replacing the 'nduja with a smoky dried chile like a chipotle morita.

For the sauce, using good-quality rice vinegar, soy sauce, and sesame oil will make all the difference. I use a darker, more powerful sesame oil for cooking, and a lighter one in the sauce.

As with any dumpling, don't get frustrated if the first ones look a bit wonky, and don't be tempted to put too much filling inside.

SERVES 2 AS A MAIN (12 DUMPLINGS)
RESTING TIME 30 MINUTES   FOLDING TIME 25 MINUTES   COOKING TIME 25 MINUTES

EINKORN WITH
FRIED FENNEL AND LUPINADE

INGREDIENTS

FOR THE EINKORN

5 oz. (140 g) einkorn,
   soaked for 12 hours
4 tbsp. olive oil
1 tbsp. raw sugar
2 tbsp. fennel seeds
2 small fennel bulbs,
   peeled and cut in
   ½ in. (1 cm) slices
salt, pepper

FOR THE LUPINADE

3½ oz. (100 g) jarred
   lupin beans, rinsed
1 small garlic clove,
   crushed
2 tbsp. lemon juice
3½ tbsp. olive oil
pepper
a small handful of
   fresh mint leaves

A few years ago, I discovered fennel. Sure I knew about it, but I never ate it growing up, so I kept passing it up on market stalls. I cannot remember what prompted me to caramelize it in olive oil, but from that point on, it became what is probably my favorite vegetable. I like it raw when it is sliced thinly, but mostly I like it browned, half-fondant, half-crispy, as in the dish below.

Lupinade, a Provence recipe made from lupin beans, feels like the missing link between hummus and tapenade (olive paste). It makes good use of the all-but-forgotten lupin beans, a cheap pantry item you wouldn't at first think that you could turn into something so nice.

Put your einkorn to cook in a saucepan on medium-high heat in twice its volume of salted water and cover with a lid. If it has been soaked it should be done in 20–30 minutes. It should retain a bite and not turn mushy. Once it's done, remove the lid, add a splash of olive oil and let it cook for a couple of minutes.

Meanwhile, prepare the lupinade by blending in a food processor all the ingredients except the mint. You want to reach a spreadable paste texture, with a light grain. Add more oil if needed and finally add the mint and blend again. Keep at room temperature until serving.

Heat the rest of the olive oil in a nonstick pan, add the sugar, the fennel seeds, and the fennel. Season with salt and pepper. Cover and leave to cook on high heat for a few minutes until it starts to caramelize. Lower the heat, flip the slices, and cover again. Leave it to cook for 10–15 minutes, until all the slices are light brown with crispy brown bits. Add more oil along the way if it starts to stick.

When ready to serve, spoon the einkorn onto shallow plate, top with the fennel and a big spoonful of lupinade.

If needed, both the einkorn and the lupinade can be made in advance. Since soaking einkorn is always a bit of a hassle, I tend to double the amount to have some for another meal. You can also skip the soaking and let it cook longer—it will be a little less digestible but still fine. Lupinade keeps well; you can use it as a spread on toasted bread or eat with a tomato salad.

Jarred lupin (also sold as lupini) beans are already salty so the lupinade should not need any extra salt.

If you can't find einkorn, try replacing it with a whole cereal like brown rice or polenta.

SERVES 2 AS A MAIN
COOKING TIME   30 MINUTES   PLUS 12 HOURS (SOAKING)
OR 45 MINUTES (WITHOUT SOAKING)

FONDANT
AU CHOCOLAT

INGREDIENTS

6½ oz. (185 g) dark
   chocolate
4½ oz. (130 g) butter,
   softened
2¾ oz. (75 g) unrefined
   dark brown
3 eggs, yolks and
   whites divided
2 tbsp. corn starch
a pinch of fine salt

A version of this recipe was acquired a long time ago by my mother. She had befriended the lover of a chocolatier who one day confided his secret recipe to her. I guess that's the ultimate form of French pillow talk and in my mind this always gave a forbidden air to the recipe.

Chocolate cakes were a staple of my mother's kitchen and I can't count the number of times I've licked melted chocolate off a bowl as a child. This particular fondant recipe was deemed fancier than the others and was made when we had guests. It was served with crème anglaise, in a picture-perfect rendition of a classic French dessert. These days, I'm much more content with serving it with thick Greek yogurt and fruit to bring a welcome kick of acidity to the plate. Unrefined sugar has also replaced the white sugar of the '90s, and has been greatly reduced. I like the caramel depth it brings to the chocolate taste.

Pre-heat your oven to 300 °F (150 °C).

Slowly melt your chocolate, either with a bain-marie or by microwaving it at a very low setting. Transfer it to a bowl and mix it with the softened butter. Add the sugar, the egg yolks, and finally the corn starch.

Add a pinch of fine salt to your egg whites and whip them into firm peaks with an electric mixer. Using a wooden spatula, progressively fold the egg whites into the chocolate mix.

Transfer to a lightly buttered cake pan with a rubber spatula, sprinkle with fleur de sel and bake for 20 minutes. This should be slightly undercooked compared to a regular cake.

Serve at room temperature or cold, alone or with strawberries and a spoonful of Greek yogurt.

Chocolate is everything to this recipe. Choose a chocolate that is not destined for baking but one that you would definitely eat by the square. At least 70 percent cocoa is a good starting point, but be guided by taste more than by percentage.

My mother had a rule that you should not open the oven while a cake with egg whites is cooking, so resist the temptation to check on it until the last minute. Eaten at room temperature, the fondant has more of a mousse texture. If you put it in the fridge it becomes more silky. Both options are nice.

FOR A ROUND 10 IN. (24 CM) CAKE PAN
PREPARATION TIME   15 MINUTES
COOKING TIME   20 MINUTES

THE MESSY, FLOWERY CHARM OF
THE EARLY DAYS OF SPRING AS
WITNESSED IN THE HAVEN OF THE
QADISHA VALLEY IN LEBANON.

1   Improvised plum clafoutis cooked in a village house in Batroun.

2   Hidden away from the chaos of Beirut, the valley is filled with olive trees and ancient monasteries.

3   Shopping at the local grocery store.

2

HOW COULD ONE NOT MARVEL AT THE
FIRST BLOOMS, THE TINIEST LEAVES
AND THE FRAGILE NEW BRANCHES THAT
HOLD THEM?

1   As early as February, white flowers start to dot the countryside—first the wild almond trees, followed by the numerous fruit trees filling the orchards.

2   A freshly picked branch of rock buckthorn and its delicate baby leaves.

2

THE GOLDEN LIGHT THAT BREAKS THROUGH
THE LAST OF THE WINTER CLOUDS HAS
AN UNMISTAKABLE NEW DAWN AIR TO IT.
SUDDENLY, THE WORLD LOOKS YOUNG AGAIN.

1   In the maquis, wild grass and twisted branches glistening in the sun.

2   Spring showers washing winter away to reveal a greener landscape.

LATE

SPRING

Here, the dizzying charm of spring probably lies in the fact that it feels impossible to partake in all that it has to offer. The memory of winter is still fresh and one hasn't settled into the abundance just yet, making that green rush absolutely mesmerizing. New wildflowers appear and disappear seemingly overnight in a tireless ballet of fresh blooms. On some days, the entire countryside fills with dandelion fluff floating in the air, glistening in the sun like in some fairy tale. All these marvels feel terribly fleeting and as the season disappears in a flash, you're left wanting more and ever-fantasizing about the next spring.

On the market stalls, many long-awaited products appear simultaneously. Peas of all sorts, zucchini, fava beans, artichokes... They all play together nicely and mixing them freely mirrors the generous nature of the season. To me, this is a season of clean, green taste. I rejoice at the idea of steamed greens with barely more than olive oil and fleur de sel, and the recipes reflect that sentiment.

PANZANELLA
PRIMAVERA

INGREDIENTS

5 tbsp. olive oil
1 small garlic clove,
   crushed
1 small zucchini, thinly
   sliced in ribbons
   with a mandoline
14 oz. (400 g) spring
   greens (snow peas,
   fava beans, peas,
   asparagus), peeled
   and ready to be
   steamed
a dozen sage leaves
3 medium slices of
   open-crumb bread
   such as ciabatta or
   sourdough, diced in
   1 in. (3 cm) chunks
¾ oz. (20 g) pine nuts
1 small mozzarella di
   bufala (4½ oz./125 g),
   shredded in rough
   pieces
a few thin slices of spicy
   sausage such as
   spianata piccante
salt, pepper
a few sage flowers
   (optional)

This is a very loose interpretation of a classic Italian panzanella, the traditional one being made with tomatoes, onions, stale bread, and vinegar. The addition of bread and mozzarella makes for a more hearty salad and recreates the very pleasing feeling of mopping up the bottom of a salad bowl with a piece of bread. This is a bit of a decadent twist on steamed spring greens. I think the clean, fresh taste of the steamed vegetables nicely compliments the richer, smokier taste of the fried bread, sage, and sausage, while the mozzarella serves as a link between them.

In a large serving bowl, mix 3 tablespoons of olive oil with the crushed garlic. Add the sliced zucchini.

Arrange the spring greens in a steam basket. Keep the ones with the same cooking time together and, if you're using snow peas, wait until the last minute to put them in. Fava beans require peeling after cooking so I generally cook them first, alone in their basket.

Put your steaming water to heat and add the baskets as you go. The vegetables should remain slightly firm. As soon as they're done, run them under cold water to stop further cooking. Don't worry about keeping them hot or cold. This recipe is great at room temperature. Add the cooked vegetables to the mixing bowl as you go along. Season with salt and pepper to taste.

Heat the remaining 2 tablespoons of olive oil in a non-stick pan, add the sage leaves followed by the bread chunks. Wait a couple of minutes until they gain color, then add your pine nuts. Keep your eyes on it because pine nuts can burn quickly. As soon as they get brown, transfer the contents of the pan to your mixing bowl.

Add the shredded mozzarella and the spianata piccante, and mix gently.

Serve in large bowls and top with a few sage flowers.

Raw garlic tastes much stronger than cooked. Pick a very small clove to start.

Raw zucchini works best with small and freshly picked specimens. They should have few seeds and ooze a bit of water when you cut them.

I vary this recipe according to whatever spring greens are available at the time. If you make it a bit earlier in the season, broccoli or romanesco work great too.

Sage leaves can be a bit challenging to find in stores—I find it's easier to grow them. Note that they keep very well in a closed box in the fridge. Basil is also a good alternative.

If you want to skip the meat, try adding a few flakes of a smoky chile (such as chipotle morita) in the bread's cooking oil.

This kind of salad benefits from being mixed some time before serving, so the flavors have time to develop. This will make the bread less crispy; you have to find the balance you prefer.

SERVES 2 AS A LIGHT MEAL
COOKING TIME 5–10 MINUTES

SWEET GREENS
SALAD

INGREDIENTS

17½ oz. (500 g) (unpeeled
    weight) fava beans
12¼ oz. (350 g) (unpeeled
    weight) peas, peeled
1 small garlic clove,
    peeled and crushed
4 tbsp. olive oil
half a small fennel
    head, thinly sliced
    with a mandoline
2 tbsp. tender golden
    raisins
a handful of
    basil leaves, torn
salt, pepper

Peas and fava beans do require a bit of peeling and patience. To my mind, the work they call for, combined with their delicate taste, makes the idea of this salad rather luxurious. Every plate like this is an act of revenge for all the canned peas I ate as a kid, unaware that another world was possible.

Put your fava beans and peas to cook in separate steam baskets. Once cooked but still rather firm (it will take a few minutes), take them out and rinse under cold water to stop the cooking.

Shell the fava beans, discarding their white outer skins.

In a salad bowl, mix the crushed garlic with the olive oil. Add the strained peas, fava beans, fennel, raisins, and basil leaves. Season with salt and pepper to taste. Serve at room temperature.

If you don't have a steam basket, you can boil the vegetables instead–just cook them separately.

If you can't find tender raisins, soak them for a few minutes in boiling water so they plump up.

For a more hearty meal, eat with a tartine of fresh goat's cheese topped with olive oil and honey.

SERVES 2 AS A LIGHT MEAL
COOKING TIME 5–10 MINUTES

1

TO HOLD THE BRIGHT GREENS OF
SPRING PRODUCE, A PALETTE OF SOFTER
ONES: BLUE, GRAY, AND KHAKI,
AS TENDER AS THE FRESH ALMOND.

1   The delicate green hue of wild sedum at their most succulent.

2   Freely mixing celadon and sage-colored ceramics.

VEGETARIAN
PAELLA

INGREDIENTS

4 tsp. olive oil
1 big garlic clove, crushed
2 tsp. paprika powder
1 small zucchini,
    cut in ⅕in. (½cm)
    slices
3 small purple artichokes,
    peeled and cut in ⅕in.
    (½cm) slices
1 small red bell pepper
    (fresh or canned),
    cut in strips
1 ripe tomato, diced
5½oz. (160g) red rice
salt, pepper
a few basil leaves, torn

Managing to find good meat-free options outside big cities is often a challenge when you travel. But for all the times you only get average alternatives, there are a few that lead to great discoveries. Paella was de rigueur for dinner at a small hotel near Granada I stayed in and I was pretty surprised to be offered a vegetarian version, and even more surprised when I tasted it. The dish below is a less spectacular recreation of that memory, and a loose variation on traditional paella, but an easy and tasty one. It's a great way to give depth to spring and summer vegetables. The vegetable combination below is my favorite but it's also great with red peppers and cumin seeds.

Heat the olive oil in a non-stick skillet. Add the garlic and paprika powder, and mix. Add the vegetables, except the tomato. Cover and leave on medium-high heat for a few minutes, until it gains some color.

Add the tomato, salt, and pepper. Mix and let it simmer for a few minutes, allowing the tomato to break down. Add the rice, mixing everything well. Add water according to the rice's cooking instructions, and an extra pinch of salt. Cover and leave to cook on medium heat for the time needed for the rice, checking on it occasionally and adding a bit of water or lowering the heat if it sticks. The rice should be cooked but retain a bite.

When the rice is done, remove the lid and leave to cook on high heat for a couple of minutes. This will make the bottom layer a bit crispy, a bit like a tahdig.

Serve in a shallow bowl with the basil leaves and a splash of good olive oil.

Red rice is very flavorful, which allows the seasoning to remain rather simple. Depending on the variety and whether it's pre-cooked, cooking time can take between 12 and 45 minutes. I always uset a little bit less water than is required and keep the rest on the side, adding it only if it sticks—you don't want to have mushy rice!

If you're using pre-cooked rice, let the vegetables cook for at least 10 minutes before adding the rice, so they can gain flavor.

This also works great with white basmati rice, in which case I would suggest a bit more paprika and even some peperoncino.

SERVES 2 AS A MAIN
COOKING TIME   25–45 MINUTES (DEPENDING ON RICE VARIETY)

2

THE DAY OF THE FIRST COURGETTES
IS A SIGN THAT SPRING IS IN FULL
SWING. FLOWERS ARE TURNED INTO
BEIGNETS IMMEDIATELY AND THE
FIRM, STICKY FLESH WILL BE AT ITS
BEST RAW OR BARELY COOKED.

1   A view in the kitchen on market day.

2   A crate of multicolored courgettes sitting on the terrace.

FRESH HERB
LASAGNA

INGREDIENTS

FOR THE
TOMATO SAUCE

3 tbsp. olive oil
1 big garlic clove,
    crushed
2½ lb. (1 kg) ripe
    tomatoes
1 tbsp. raw sugar
1 small peperoncino,
    crushed
salt, pepper

FOR THE
BROUSSE FILLING

14 oz. (400 g) brousse
    or ricotta
½ cup (140 ml) milk
1¾ oz. (50 g) roughly
    grated Parmigiano-
    Reggiano, plus ¾ oz.
    (20 g) for dusting
pepper
a handful of fresh herbs,
    roughly chopped
    (savory, basil)

5¼ oz. (150 g)
    lasagna sheets

Growing up with average versions of lasagna drenched in béchamel I became a bit ambivalent about the Italian staple. I guess this story took a turn when I ordered fresh brousse lasagna in a tiny mountain restaurant in Corsica. It tasted as light as a cloud, and there was no béchamel in sight—finally a version I could get behind! In the recipe below, I have added tomato sauce layers but kept the simple, fresh spirit of the original.

Start with the tomato sauce. Heat the olive oil in a large saucepan and fry the garlic until slightly golden. Add the rest of the ingredients, bring to a simmer on high heat, then cover and lower the heat. You don't want the sauce to reduce too much because the lasagna sheets will need the humidity. Cook for 15 minutes. To smooth the sauce, either use a mouli or a blender (be careful if it's still hot).

Meanwhile, prepare the brousse filling. In a bowl, mix the brousse and the milk with a fork and add cheese, pepper, and herbs.

Pre-heat your oven to 350 °F (180 °C).

Oil the bottom of an 8 × 11 in. (20 × 28 cm) oven dish. Add a first layer of lasagna sheets, without overlapping them. Start with a brousse layer and alternate with tomato, doing two layers of each, finishing with tomato. Sprinkle the 1¾ oz. (20 g) of grated parmigiano on top. Cover the dish with foil and bake in the oven for 25 minutes, then remove the foil and cook for 10 more minutes. Check that it's cooked with a knife. It should go in as in soft butter.

Serve with a drizzle of good olive oil on top.

High-quality lasagna sheets really make all the difference. My personal favorites are from Italian brand La Campofilone. I prefer the thinner ones, which are almost see-through when uncooked, but if yours are on the thicker side you can increase the quantity of liquid a little.

For a quicker version you can use a bottle of passata di pomodoro, around 1⅓ lb. (600 g) without pre-cooking it. I add salt, pepper, crushed garlic, a tablespoon of sugar, and a good splash of olive oil before layering it in the dish.

For a more wintry variation, try adding puréed steamed broccoli and garlic to the brousse filling.

SERVES 4 AS A MAIN
COOKING TIME   30 MINUTES

BLACK RICE WITH PESTO AND
CARAMELIZED ZUCCHINI

INGREDIENTS

FOR THE RICE

4 tbsp. olive oil
5½ oz. (160 g) black rice
1 peperoncino,
    crushed (optional)
1 garlic clove, crushed
2 small zucchini, cut
    in ⅕ in. (½ cm) slices
salt, pepper
a pinch of grated lemon
    zest (optional)

FOR THE PESTO

1¾ oz. (50 g) almonds
1¾ oz. (50 g) Parmigiano-
    Reggiano, diced
1 small garlic clove,
    roughly chopped
a handful of basil leaves,
    plus more to serve
olive oil

I used to take zucchini for granted. It was always a staple of my mother's cooking, and I would buy them all year round in Paris without thinking twice. Here in the south, they're ubiquitous for long months, but they do disappear somewhere in the fall, leaving us longing for their versatility and sweet taste. I now welcome the first zucchini of the year with a sigh of relief because when they're here, it feels like we're officially out of trouble weather-wise.
This recipe gives them the decadent welcome they deserve. I find this combination to be especially delicious, with the added benefit of feeling very fancy without requiring any hard work.

Heat 1 tablespoon of the olive oil in a pot. Add the rice and coat the grains for a minute. Add two times the volume of rice in water. Cover and let it simmer on medium heat until the rice is done, following the instructions on the package.

Meanwhile, prepare the pesto. Toast the almonds in a hot pan until they're slightly brown. Add them to your blender with the parmigiano and the small garlic clove. Grind to a medium-fine powder. Add a pinch of salt and pepper, the basil leaves, and a splash of olive oil. Mix again. Continue adding more oil until you have the consistency of a spreadable paste. Put aside.

Heat the remaining 3 tablespoons of olive oil in a non-stick pan, add the crushed peperoncino and garlic, then wait a minute before adding the zucchini. Add salt and pepper, cover and leave on high heat for a few minutes, allowing the zucchini to brown. Lower the heat and leave to cook for around 8 minutes, until soft but not mushy.

When the rice is ready, switch off the heat and mix the pesto into it.

Serve in a bowl, topped with the zucchini, a few basil leaves, and the lemon zest, if using.

Black rice generally takes a while to cook but is well worth the wait.

This pesto is light on basil, so it doesn't overpower the taste of the black rice. If you want it a bit greener, you can add a handful of spinach sprouts.

SERVES 2 AS A MAIN
COOKING TIME 45 MINUTES (DEPENDING ON RICE VARIETY)

GRILLED ZUCCHINI AND
PECORINO SALAD

INGREDIENTS

1 zucchini, thinly
    sliced lengthwise
    with a mandoline
6 tbsp. olive oil
2 slices of rye bread, cut
    in ½ in. (1.5 cm) cubes
1 tbsp. fennel seeds
1 tbsp. white balsamic
    vinegar
half a fennel head,
    thinly sliced
    with a mandoline
1 small crunchy
    apple, thinly sliced
1 tbsp. soft golden raisins
1¾ oz. (50 g) pecorino
    pepato, cut in ½ in.
    (1 cm) chunks
a few basil leaves, torn
salt, pepper

Most of our dinners revolve around a salad of some sort. In truth, I rarely ever cook the exact same one and always like to take a small chance with a new combination, even if it's just a twist on the herbs. This particular recipe has a winter base—fennel and apples are ingredients I rely on a lot during the cold months—but it's rejuvenated by the addition of strips of young zucchini. With the arrival of spring, it's tempting to forget all about the tired staples that have gotten us through winter, but as it turns out, like us, they just need a bit of spring energy to feel brand new again. Here the sweet and salty combination, carried by the smoky depth of rye bread, is really satisfying.

Heat up a non-stick skillet or grill pan and add your zucchini in a single layer. Add salt and pepper and cook until colored but still a bit firm. Put aside on a plate once done.

Heat 3 tablespoons of olive oil in a pan (you can use the same as the zucchini), and cook your rye bread and fennel seeds for 5 minutes, stirring, until golden.

In a large mixing bowl, mix 3 tablespoons of olive oil with the balsamic vinegar. Add the fennel, apple, raisins, pecorino, basil, and, finally, the grilled zucchini. Add salt and pepper to taste, mix gently, and serve immediately.

White balsamic vinegar, the lesser-known cousin of black balsamic, has won my heart with its honey-like sweetness. I find it rather versatile, be it in dressings or on grilled eggplant, a dish I had once in a Ligurian trattoria.

If you can't find pecorino pepato, try Manchego or any semi-hard ewe's cheese.

SERVES 2 AS A LIGHT MEAL
COOKING TIME 5–10 MINUTES

RHUBARB, PISTACHIO, AND SEMOLINA CAKE

INGREDIENTS

5 oz. (140 g) butter, softened, plus extra for greasing

4¼ oz. (120 g) golden sugar

4¼ oz. (120 g) medium semolina

5¼ oz. (150 g) unsalted pistachios, finely ground

a pinch of salt

1 tsp. baking powder

1 egg

4 tbsp. Greek yogurt

1 tbsp. orange blossom water

14 oz. (400 g) rhubarb, peeled and cut in ½ in. (1 cm) cubes

I've adored fruit ever since I was a child, but rhubarb was my nemesis. I couldn't understand why my mother kept making pies, jams, and compotes out of it when there was an infinity of other delicious fruits to pick from. My grandmother had this old rhubarb plant in her garden that kept giving and giving every year without fault. Years with cherries on the family tree were few and far between, but you could bet that old rhubarb plant would always bear fruit. It still does to this day and now I'm glad, since somewhere on the path to adulthood I began to love the taste of rhubarb.

I've got such a soft spot for Middle Eastern pastries: the rich nutty flavors, the floral perfumes, the sophisticated textures ... But they're so sugary that I don't eat them often and can't bring myself to bake them according to their original recipes because of the huge amount of sugar. This recipe, while still being rather indulgent, feels like a good compromise. The rhubarb brings the moisture usually provided by a syrup and a slight touch of acidity to a crumbly and fondant semolina base.

Pre-heat your oven to 350 °F (180 °C).

Using a whisk, mix the softened butter in a bowl and the sugar until pale and creamy.

In a separate bowl, mix the semolina, ground pistachios, salt, and baking powder before adding it to the butter and sugar and whisking again. Add the egg, mix, then add the yogurt and orange blossom water and stir until the batter is homogenous. Finally, add the rhubarb cubes and mix gently.

Lightly grease the cake pan and dust the base and sides with a bit of sugar. Pour the batter into the prepared pan and level the top with a rubber spatula. Smooth the surface and put in the oven for 40 minutes, or until the middle has a nice, medium-brown color.

The cake is fragile while hot, so wait until it has cooled down before removing it from the cake pan.

This recipe calls for the size of semolina that would be used for couscous, not the fine one often used for pastries. Or you can use regular flour instead, the cake will be more like a fondant.

If you don't have pistachio this would also be nice with almonds or walnuts.

I first tasted real orange blossom water in Lebanon. Before that, I didn't know that most of what is sold is a synthetic reproduction of the real thing. Once you've tasted it, there's no going back! Learn to read the labels and stay away from anything that says aroma.

The cake will keep on the counter for a couple of days but due to the presence of fruit it's best to put it in the fridge to keep it longer.

FOR A 1½ IN. (4 CM) HIGH CAKE IN A
10 IN. (24 CM) ROUND CAKE PAN OR 8 IN. (21 CM) SQUARE PAN
COOKING TIME   40 MINUTES

1

IN THE HEYDAY OF SPRING,
IT SEEMS THERE IS A NEW KIND OF
WILDFLOWER BLOOMING EVERYDAY,
THE BRIGHTEST OF YELLOW
BEING THEIR COLOR OF CHOICE.

1   A vibrant bouquet featuring wild euphorbias.

2   For a brief moment, the discreet sedums rise above the ground and burst into the brightest flowers.

2

CELEBRATING A TIME FOR NATURE
TO RUN FREE, THE JOY OF BEING
SWEPT AWAY IN A GLORIOUS REALM
OF WEEDS AND HAPPILY OVERRUN
BY A FLURRY OF NEWBORN LEAVES.

1   The hazy glow of the silver-tipped olive leaves make for enchanting pastoral scenes.

2   Foraging heaps of wildflowers to turn into a collection of ephemeral bouquets.

EARLY

SUMMER

If spring is about a dizzying, mild hysteria, early summer is already an invitation to start to slow down as nature settles into a sunny, bountiful mode. Gone is the dread of cold days, warmth is here to stay, announcing what feels like a never-ending season.

I used to fantasize about what I'd do on these balmy summer nights—perhaps sit in contemplation on the terrace as the heat goes from intense to sweet. Instead, in these hours before real darkness, it sometimes feels like a whole new day is starting, and I find myself out and about, often with scissors in hand, leaving the house on a whim to pick wildflowers as the sky turns red. When I come back and arrange them in the feeble light of a sun that just won't quit, I feel the thrill of this endless dusk; it's the taste of stolen time.

Before long, the humming of the bees in the lavender fields fills the air. We won't taste that particular honey for a few weeks, but the long-awaited spring-flowers honey is finally arriving. In the market, tomato season has really started and it's hard to resist putting them in every dish. With them come the cherries, the apricots, and the peppers, playing along with the last of the spring greens.

TACOS,
SPANISH-STYLE

FOR THE TORTILLAS

2 oz. (60 g) all-purpose
　flour
2 oz. (60 g) einkorn
　flour
1 tsp. salt
¼ cup (60 ml) water
2 tbsp. olive oil

FOR THE SALSA

1 fleshy tomato
1 small red chili,
　deseeded and thinly
　chopped
2 spring onions, finely
　chopped
a handful of coriander
　sprigs, finely chopped
a piece of sweet red
　pepper, finely diced
3 tbsp. olive oil
salt, pepper

FOR THE GUACAMOLE

1 tbsp. coriander seeds
1 avocado
juice of half a lime
3 tbsp. olive oil
salt, pepper

1¾ oz. (50 g) hard
　ewe's cheese such as
　Manchego, grated
12 thin spicy
　chorizo slices
　(optional)

Early summer sees our first dinners outside, with the orange sunset light and perfumed air that will be the hallmark of the evenings to come.
Most of the ingredients required by Mexican cuisine can only remain a distant fantasy where I live. Still, I find it extremely inspiring and wanted to recreate a taco recipe that would draw its inspiration from Spain, a land I know better, and that I could easily make every day. I think what makes this otherwise rather simple combination of ingredients so tasty is that everything is made from scratch. This turns it into something satisfying and special, and so does the table laid out with all the toppings. It's a bit of work, but the outcome makes it worthwhile.

Prepare the tortilla dough. In a bowl, mix the flours and salt and make a well at the center, adding the water and the oil then mixing it with a fork. Knead with your hands for a couple of minutes before forming a ball. Cover and leave to rest while you prepare the rest.

Prepare the salsa, so the flavors have some time to infuse. Grate the tomato and strain so it has a purée texture. Don't discard the juice. Drink it or save it for a salad dressing. Add the rest of the salsa ingredients and mix thoroughly. Put in a serving bowl and leave at room temperature.

For the guacamole, start by toasting the coriander seeds in a pan until fragrant, then roughly grind them in a mortar. Peel your avocado on a cutting board, crush it with a fork, and fold the rest of the ingredients in. You want the texture to remain a bit uneven.

At this point you can start putting the salsa, guacamole, and cheese, all in separate bowls, on the table.

Heat up a flat pan on very high heat. While it's heating, divide your dough into 6 even-sized balls on a lightly floured surface and start spreading them into about 8 in. (20 cm)-wide discs with a rolling pin. Cook them as you spread them, transferring them to a serving plate as you go. Cook for 2–3 minutes, waiting until bubbles form at the surface before flipping them. They should color only slightly in places.

Once you're done with the tortillas, quickly grill the chorizo in the same pan. It should only take a minute if the slices are really thin.

Bring the tortillas and the chorizo to the table and let everyone fill their own tacos.

I often play around with the flours, keeping at least a third of regular wheat flour so it's easy to roll out but otherwise making blue corn, spelt, buckwheat or whole wheat variations. Try adding a teaspoon of turmeric powder to the dough for a beautiful contrast with the filling.

If I wanted to make larger quantities or do corn tortillas, whose dough is more delicate to handle, I would probably use a tortilla press. With this recipe and these quantities you're fine without it.

Replacing the water with milk will make the tortilla softer, but I like them to retain a slight crunch.

I like to keep the guacamole fresh and simple to let the salsa shine.

I usually keep a few quarters of lime on the table to add some extra kick to each taco.

SERVES 2 AS A MAIN
PREPPING TIME　40 MINUTES
COOKING TIME　10 MINUTES

MEDITERRANEAN CHIRASHI
WITH CRISP GREENS AND SALSA VERDE

INGREDIENTS

FOR THE CHIRASHI

5¼ oz. (150 g)
　　Japanese rice such
　　as koshihikari
salt
1 tbsp. rice vinegar
1 tsp. agave syrup
2 handfuls fava beans,
　　peeled
half an avocado
7 oz. (200 g) raw
　　salmon, skin removed
3 spring onions, white
　　parts, finely sliced
2 pink radishes, finely
　　sliced

FOR THE SALSA VERDE

a small bunch of
　　coriander sprigs
juice of half a lime
3 spring onions, green
　　parts
1 small garlic clove,
　　grated
2 tbsp. tamari soy sauce
7 tbsp. olive oil
½ tsp. wasabi (optional)

We rarely eat fish, and raw fish in particular feels like a luxury. It reminds me of Japan and one trip where, going from one ryokan meal to the next, it felt as though we were eating seafood at every meal. For a while I was intimidated by the idea of preparing chirashi but once you've gathered quality ingredients it's actually rather straightforward and quick to put together. I also appreciate the fact that you buy much smaller quantities of fish per person with this kind of recipe than with a classic dish where it is cooked. This feels more responsible and means you have the opportunity to opt for a much better quality of fish. This Mediterranean variation puts the greens forward and plays on the surprisingly good combination of olive oil and soy sauce.

Rinse your rice under cold water until the water runs clear. If you have time, let it soak for up to 30 minutes.

Drain it well before putting it in a saucepan with a little less than twice its volume in water (one and a half if it has soaked). Add a pinch of coarse salt, cover, and bring to a simmer. Let it cook on medium heat for 10 minutes.

Meanwhile, mix the vinegar and the agave syrup in a small cup.

Put the fava beans to cook in a steam basket. In a few minutes they should be softer but still a little firm. Rinse them under cold water and remove the outer skins, keeping only the tender part. Put aside.

Once the rice is done, add the vinegar-agave mix and stir gently with a wooden spoon. If you're eating right away, you can divide it directly into shallow bowls. Otherwise cover and put aside.

Mix the salsa ingredients in a food processor until you have a loose green sauce.

Cut the avocado and salmon in slices.

Lay all the ingredients in the bowls over the rice, finishing with the sauce. If you want, put the extra sauce in a small pitcher to add as you eat.

I find it's worth looking for high-quality Japanese rice from specialty stores. The same goes for having a good bottle of tamari soy sauce (the one you use for dressings, rather than cooking).

Fava beans aren't a bestseller on French market stalls, unlike in northern Africa. I suspect it's because they need to be peeled twice, once when they're raw and once when they're cooked.

Good salmon is easy to find here, but if you have access to fatty tuna, scallops, or sea bream, these work great, or even better. If you're new to preparing raw fish, I would suggest starting with salmon.

Cutting fish easily requires a sharp knife. No need to buy a huge knife if you're not used to these. There are smaller Japanese ones available.

CRISPY ARTICHOKES
ON SALSA CRUDA

INGREDIENTS

1 large, ripe red tomato
1 small garlic clove,
    grated
4 small purple artichokes
half a lemon
4 tbsp. olive oil
salt, pepper
1 mozzarella di bufala ball
    (4½ oz./125 g),
    torn
a few basil leaves,
    torn
focaccia or ciabatta,
    to serve

I find the sophistication of purple artichokes hard to resist. Like all refined things, they tend to be elusive and require a bit of work, but for them I'm willing to jump through a few hoops. Here in Provence, they make a surprise appearance on market stalls sometimes quite early in the winter. This kicks off what feels like a hide-and-seek season that lingers until the early fall. When their presence magically aligns with perfectly red and ripe summer tomatoes, I jump at the opportunity to cook this simple yet luxurious dish.

Grate your tomato in a wide bowl. You want it to be a bit thicker than a gazpacho, so remove some liquid if needed. Add salt, pepper, and garlic. Divide it between two shallow plates and leave at room temperature while you prepare the rest.

Start peeling the artichokes. Remove two layers of leaves before discarding the tip of the bud and starting to peel the stem and remaining bud until it's light green and tender. Cut it in half and discard the hairy center if there is one. Squeeze lemon juice on it so it doesn't darken and continue to peel all of them. When they are all ready, cut them thinly in ⅛ in. (½ cm) slices and cook them immediately.

Heat up the olive oil in a non-stick pan then add the artichokes, along with salt and pepper. Stir to coat them in oil, cover, and leave to cook on medium-high heat for a few minutes. They should be tender and crispy. Add more oil if you feel they're too dry and remove the lid if they don't color enough.

Place the fried artichokes on top of the salsa cruda, along with a few bits of torn mozzarella and basil leaves. Add a generous splash of good olive oil and serve with a focaccia or ciabatta.

Finding excellent, sweet, fleshy tomatoes is essential.

This recipe calls for small, spiny, purple artichokes. I hardly ever eat the globe ones, whose taste I find a bit bland.

When you prepare artichokes, it is common to put them in lemon water as you go. In this recipe, since we are only making a few and we are frying them, we want them to be as dry as possible.

SERVES 2 AS A LIGHT MEAL
COOKING TIME 5–10 MINUTES

LEMONY GREEN
TABBOULEH

INGREDIENTS

FOR THE TABBOULEH

2½ oz. (70 g) medium
  grain semolina
3½ tbsp. boiling water
1¾ oz. (50 g) radishes,
  cut in ⅕ in. (½ cm)
  dice
5¼ oz. (150 g) cucumber,
  cut in ⅕ in. (½ cm) dice
6¼ oz. (180 g) green
  pepper, cut in ⅕ in.
  (½ cm) strips
¾ oz. (20 g) spring
  onion, thinly sliced
15 mint leaves, chopped
a few wild fennel sprigs,
  chopped
1 tbsp. golden raisins
3 tbsp. linseeds
1 tbsp. sunflower seeds
3 tbsp. almonds,
  cut lengthwise

FOR THE DRESSING

1 tsp. whole tahini
1 garlic clove, grated
juice of 1 small lemon
¾ in. (2 cm) fresh ginger,
  peeled and thinly
  grated
4 tbsp. sesame oil
2 tbsp. olive oil
2 tbsp. tamari soy sauce
salt, pepper

My mother used to turn the making of tabbouleh into a ceremonial, labor-intensive affair that confirmed the arrival of summer. It was an almost military operation, at odds with the slightly disheveled, carefree vision I now have of the dish. Every vegetable had to be chopped into tiny, regular pieces while the herbs, selected with an expert eye from the garden, were layered carefully before being cut with scissors. She would make a giant bowl of it, even if there were only three of us, and it was her pride to know that her tabbouleh was nothing like the soggy ones you could buy from the supermarket or eat from any local caterer's buffet. This was the '90s in rural eastern France and cooking with olive oil was still an eccentricity. To this day, I wonder where my mother came up with this version of a tabbouleh, one that was lighter on herbs than the original but heavy on veggies. This recipe is a very free variation on her own iteration. It is both crunchy and bright, with an extra depth brought by the soy sauce and tahini.

Put the uncooked semolina in a large mixing bowl and pour the boiling water on top. Mix with a fork and cover with a plate while you cut the vegetables, giving it some time to cook and cool down a bit.

Fluff the semolina with a fork. It will be slightly undercooked, which is normal—the water from the vegetables and the dressing will cook it through. Add the vegetables, chopped herbs, and raisins to the bowl, and mix.

Heat up a non-stick pan and grill the seeds and almonds for a few minutes until golden. Transfer to the mixing bowl.

In a small separate bowl, mix all the dressing ingredients. Add it to the mixing bowl and mix well.

You can eat it right away for a fresher, more acidic taste or leave it in the fridge for 30 minutes for a deeper taste.

The radishes can be replaced by pomegranate seeds once they're in season.

If you don't have wild fennel, you can use dill.

For this kind of recipe, I tend to favor a lighter-colored sesame oil with a more subtle taste.

SERVES 2 AS A LIGHT MEAL
COOKING TIME 5 MINUTES

2

BREAKFAST OUTSIDE IS ONE
OF THE SEASON'S TRUE LUXURIES.

1   Cantaloupe, einkorn bread, bloody peach juice, and Greek yogurt with date syrup.

2   Early morning light playing tricks with an old photo lens.

BRICK À L'OEUF
AND SWEET RED PEPPER SALAD

INGREDIENTS

FOR THE SALAD

5 tbsp. olive oil
1 tsp. cumin seeds
5 oz. (140 g) sweet red
    pepper, cut in
    ⅛ in. (½ cm) strips
10½ oz. (300 g) red
    tomatoes, deseeded
    and cut in strips
a few sprigs of fresh
    coriander, chopped
salt, pepper

FOR THE BRICK

4 tbsp. olive oil
4 square sheets
    of brick pastry
2 eggs
a handful of fresh
    coriander sprigs,
    chopped
2 spring onions, chopped
1 tbsp. coriander
    seeds, toasted and
    roughly crushed
4 tbsp. grated cheese
    such as Emmental

Cooking an egg in a folded brick pastry sheet is a staple of North African cuisine. It's a simple yet formidable idea that makes eggs fluffy and flavors them with whatever you put inside. As with any filled preparation, I find it best not to overdo it. Keep it about herbs, spices, and a bit of cheese. It's honestly good on its own but accompanied by a refined salad it becomes more than a street-food snack. The sweet and fragrant taste, and the soft textures are really hallmarks of what I love about Moroccan food. It's comforting and sophisticated at the same time.

Start with the salad. Heat 2 tablespoons of olive oil in a non-stick pan on medium heat, add the cumin seeds, followed by the pepper strips. Mix to coat, add salt and pepper, cover, and leave to cook until soft. Watch the heat as peppers tend to blacken quickly.

Meanwhile, put 3 tablespoons of olive oil in a salad bowl. Add the tomatoes, chopped coriander, salt, pepper, and finally the fried peppers. Mix again and let it sit at room temperature while you prepare the bricks.

Have all the brick ingredients ready on the counter before starting the process. The brick dough is thin and you have to act relatively quickly. Heat up the olive oil in a large flat pan on medium heat. Layer two brick pastry sheets on a shallow plate and crack one egg in the middle of each. Salt and pepper the egg before topping it with half the fresh coriander, the spring onions, the coriander seeds, and the Emmental. Fold it into a flat rectangle and flip it into the hot pan. The folded parts should be face-down. Proceed the same way for the second brick, placing it next to the other. Let them cook on medium-high heat for 5 minutes, flipping midway. They should grill and get crispy brown.

Once they're done, transfer each one to a plate and top with the pepper salad.

With red peppers, I've found that the thinner the flesh, the better. If you can find them, use the elongated varieties rather than bell peppers.

If you don't have a big enough pan to hold two bricks at the same time, you can cook them one after the other or use two smaller pans simultaneously.

SERVES 2 AS A LIGHT MEAL
COOKING TIME 15–20 MINUTES

RASPBERRY, BROUSSE, AND HONEY TARTELETTES

INGREDIENTS

5¼ oz. (150 g) raspberries

FOR THE CRUST

3 oz. (80 g) all-purpose
    flour
2 oz. (60 g)
    ground almonds
¾ oz. (20 g) unrefined
    sugar
a pinch of salt
2 oz. (60 g) butter,
    softened
2 tbsp. cold water

FOR THE CREAM

2¼ oz. (65 g) very fresh
    brousse or ricotta
1 tsp. chestnut honey
5 raspberries

My mother used to bake a fruit pie every Sunday when I was growing up, and still does. She has a strict pie etiquette which involves making your own dough, being very generous with the fruits, lining them up with care (nothing makes her frown like people recklessly "tossing fruits" on pies) and using restraint with frills such as crème pâtissière.

One of my main food obsessions is berries. I almost welcome the first strawberry with a tear in my eye, still fantasize about the mountains of blueberries sold in Transylvanian markets, and famously fell into a spiky bush of raspberries as a child. It's a craving that never seems to be fulfilled, no matter how much of them I eat. The season is always too short, the bounty too small. Out of deep love and respect for them, I like to keep berry pies rather minimalistic. This particular combination of a semi-soft almond crust and honey-flavored brousse is very easy to put together and a true delight.

First prepare the crust. In a mixing bowl, mix all the dry ingredients with a fork before adding the soft butter and water. Mix carefully with a fork, working the dough as little as possible. Form 4 even-sized balls, cover the dough with plastic wrap, and ideally put in the fridge for at least 30 minutes, which will make it easier to handle.

Pre-heat your oven to 350 °F (180 °C).

Using your fingers, carefully flatten the dough into the base of each tartelette pan to form a disk, adding a bit of flour only if it gets too sticky.

Put the tartelette pans in the oven to bake for 10 minutes. They should only slightly color on the edges, so don't be tempted to leave them in the oven any longer. Leave them to cool at room temperature before carefully turning the tartelette bases out onto 4 plates.

When ready to serve, prepare the cream by mixing all the ingredients with a spoon, crushing the 5 raspberries in the process.

Divide the cream between the tartelettes, spreading it gently on the crust. Line up your raspberries in circles, close together, and serve immediately.

If you don't have tartelette tins, you can also cut the dough in circles with a small bowl and bake them on parchment paper. You can make the pie a bit ahead of time but I find it's better to make it at the last moment—that way the cream and berries are fresh but the crust is at room temperature.

Chestnut honey has a distinct caramel flavor that works great with ricotta or brousse. It stays liquid and keeps well so it's worth having a small jar of it in the cupboard.

For this recipe you want your brousse or ricotta to be extra fresh. After a couple of days in the fridge they can develop a stronger taste that, while totally fine in savory and cooked preparations, won't work paired with fruits.

This recipe also works beautifully with strawberries.

FOR 4 TARTELETTES (3½ IN./9 CM-WIDE)
OR ONE SMALL PIE (7 IN./17 CM)
PREPPING TIME 15 MINUTES   RESTING TIME 30 MINUTES
COOKING TIME 10 MINUTES

AS SOON AS I SEE THE FIRST FLOWERS AND
HEAR THE BEES, I START TO FANTASIZE
ABOUT THE LIQUID GOLD PRODUCED BY THEM.
I LIKE A CUPBOARD FILLED WITH
HONEY FROM OUR HILLS AND WANDERLUST-
INDUCING JARS BROUGHT FROM OTHER
CORNERS OF THE WORLD.

1　Einkorn bread topped with butter and maquis honey is my breakfast tartine of choice since living in Provence.

2　I use lighter honeys in cakes and granolas and eat the stronger ones raw.

APRICOT AND DOCE DE LEITE ICE CREAM
WITH PISTACHIO MACAROONS

INGREDIENTS

FOR A SMALL
JAR OF DOCE DE LEITE

2 cups (500 ml) full-fat
    milk
7 oz. (200 g) golden
    sugar

FOR 15 SMALL
MACAROONS

1 egg white
a pinch of fine salt
1 oz. (25 g) golden sugar
3½ oz. (100 g) ground
    pistachios

FOR THE ICE CREAM

10 oz. (275 g) ripe
    apricots, pitted
2 oz. (55 g) doce de
    leite
2 tbsp. lemon juice

I discovered Portugal and its food rather late. In my defense, a Portuguese woman once told me that they too often fail to advertise what they have to offer. This humble disposition makes their sincere, no-frills cooking all the more enticing to me. We once spent a few days on an organic farm that doubled as a small hotel, called Companhia das Culturas, where the food was especially great. Jossara, the cook, quickly became my favorite person as she fed me one marvel after another. I got obsessed with her apricot ice cream, and, as I was asking for yet another bowl of it, she took me to her stash and let me in on the secret: besides using organic Algarve apricots from the farm, she was mixing them with doce de leite—sweet, condensed milk.
Macaroons are the fantastic consequence of making yolk-heavy recipes like flan. They provide a sweet answer to the question of what to do with the egg whites. I've reduced the amount of sugar a lot compared to traditional recipes, which makes them more about the nuts. They're the perfect companion to ice cream and will also make for a decadent sweet sandwich if filled with whipped cream and berries.

First make the doce de leite. Put the milk and sugar in a saucepan and let it cook on medium heat, checking on it regularly, for 30 minutes. When ready, it should have reduced by half, thickened into a loose paste, and turned a light-gold color. If you leave it longer it will darken and have a stronger caramel taste, which might overshadow the apricot taste. Put it in a jar and leave to cool at room temperature.

Make the macaroons. Pre-heat your oven to 280°F (140°C). Add the salt to your egg white and whip it to firm peaks with an electric mixer. Add the sugar and keep mixing until well incorporated. With a wooden spoon gently fold in the pistachios.

Line a baking tray with parchment paper. Using a pastry bag or a tablespoon, pipe or spoon 15 macaroons onto the lined baking tray. Bake in the oven for 18 minutes. They should only color slightly and remain chewy inside once cooled down. Once out of the oven, gently lift them from the parchment paper with a spatula and put them to cool on a wire cooling rack.

Finally, assemble the ice cream. Put the apricots, doce de leite, and lemon juice in the bowl of a stand mixer and mix until smooth. Taste for sweetness and add more doce de leite if necessary. You can also add more lemon juice if your apricots lack a bit of flavor. Put the mix in the fridge for at least 1 hour—it's best to put already cold ingredients into the ice-cream machine. Churn the ice cream in an ice-cream maker, following the manufacturer's instructions, for about 40 minutes.

When ready to serve, crumble a few macaroons on the ice cream and enjoy right away.

You can, of course, use ready-made, condensed milk, but it's easy enough to make it yourself if you want to skip the industrial version.

For this recipe you want the apricots to be ripe and soft.

If you don't have an ice-cream maker, this mixture will make nice popsicles.

Egg whites, unlike egg yolks, will keep in the fridge for several days.

SERVES 4
FOR THE DOCE DE LEITE: COOKING TIME 30 MINUTES   COOL-DOWN TIME 1 HOUR
FOR THE ICE CREAM: COOL-DOWN TIME 2 HOURS
CHURNING TIME 40 MINUTES (DEPENDING ON THE MACHINE)
FOR THE MACAROONS: COOKING TIME 18 MINUTES

NATURE AT ITS MOST GRACIOUS UNDER
THE GOLDEN LIGHT OF THE SOLSTICE.

1   A young lamb grazing in a village nearby.

2   Our dry garden at its peak, with fluffy bushes undulating with the warm summer wind.

2

IN THIS CORNER OF PROVENCE, LAVENDER
FIELDS BLOOM DURING THE LONGEST DAYS
OF THE YEAR. AT SUNSET, THE WARMED-UP
FLOWERS FILL THE AIR WITH PERFUME
WHILE THEIR HUE STAINS THE SKY, GIVING
BIRTH TO ENDLESS PURPLE DUSKS.

1   Coming back home with a fragrant late-evening bounty of lavender, vine leaves, and wildflowers.

2   Wild oats light up the disheveled lavender fields around our house, offering cues on potential bouquets.

LATE

SUMMER

The first summer I spent here was like something out of a storybook. It took me back to the feeling I had as a child during the summer break, one of carefree holidays where each hot and sunny day starts to blur into the next. Here, you could easily let yourself lose track of time, hypnotized by the sound of the cicadas, a rhythm that feels deafening at first, before turning into the telling sign of the hottest hours of the day. When they stop in the evening, it's as if everything that has been slowly baking in the sun gently releases its perfume.

As the side of the road turns to an undulating golden blanket, anything watery and refreshing starts to sound right. Flavors I might dismiss as not deep enough at any other season are suddenly all I desire. Intense sun will change your cravings as surely as merciless cold will. Any recipe requiring heat must be deemed worth the extra degrees and compete with the appeal of eating everything raw.

It's a time when the boundary between fruits and vegetables seems to disappear in an avalanche of improvised salads. Peaches, nectarines, and all kinds of melons are easily thrown together with the bountiful zucchini, tomatoes, and cucumbers. It's a season of carefree cooking—as it should be.

FRESH ROLLS WITH
CUCUMBER AND FENNEL

INGREDIENTS

FOR THE ROLLS

2 oz. (60 g) uncooked
  rice vermicelli
2 spring onions, finely
  chopped
5 oz. (140 g) cucumber,
  deseeded, cut in 4 in.
  (10 cm) sticks
3½ oz. (100 g) fennel,
  thinly sliced
  and chopped
1 tbsp. lemon juice
½ in. (1 cm) fresh ginger,
  grated
1 tbsp. toasted unsalted
  cashews
1 tbsp. toasted sesame
  seeds
24 small mint leaves
8 baby spinach leaves
8 rice-paper wrappers
  (7 in./18 cm wide)

FOR THE SAUCE

2 tbsp. olive oil
4 tbsp. ponzu sauce

One of my first faraway trips, quite a long time ago, was to Vietnam. Until then, Asian food had only been a flavorful cuisine whose workings were completely mysterious to me. Traveling someplace won't give you instant knowledge of a country's cooking, but seeing dishes in their context, beyond the often-standardized version imported to your home country, can shine a light on the logic behind some of its foundations. What dawned on me through many delicious Vietnamese meals, beyond the fact that everything was incredibly fresh and light, bursting with herbs and vegetables, was the genius of the rice wrapper. I realized the obvious: here was a way to make your salad portable, its packaging edible, almost putting an end to the practical supremacy of the sandwich over the salad. What also struck me was how almost everything could be eaten this way. A whole dish was presented in fragments for you to assemble in your own rolls. The variation below is fresh, crunchy, and slightly tangy—perfect for a hot summer day.

First cook the rice vermicelli. Put them in a large pot of boiling water, this should only take a couple of minutes. They should take a few minutes to cook. They need to be soft but stop the cooking before the noodles break. Drain and run under cold water. Press them into the colander with your hands to remove any excess water. Keep in the fridge while you prepare the rest.

Get all your vegetables ready on a cutting board next to each other. Add the lemon juice and grated ginger to the fennel and mix.

Prepare your station with the fillings on one side, a wooden board to prepare the rolls, a shallow plate big enough to fit wrappers filled with water, and a platter large enough to hold all the finished rolls without them touching each other.

Once ready, proceed as follows for each roll: dip your wrapper in water for a couple of seconds (you will think it's not enough but any longer and they will get too soft), lay it on the board and add the fillings in the center, leaving 1 in. (3 cm) empty on the left and right and at least 2 in. (5 cm) on the top and bottom. The order in which you place them is mostly cosmetic—for a nice effect I would suggest starting with a pinch of sesame seeds, followed by three mint leaves, fennel, cucumber, spring onions, cashews, vermicelli, and finally a spinach leaf. Fold the left and right side toward the center before rolling it tightly. The wrappers have a bit of stretch that allows that. If you make them too loose they will be messy when eaten.

Put them on the platter as you go, making sure they don't touch each other. A short time in the fridge (at least 10 minutes) will help them hold together. Just be sure to cover the platter so they don't dry out.

When ready to eat, mix the olive oil and ponzu sauce and divide between small cups to dip the rolls into.

Smaller rice-paper wrappers like these are much easier to handle than the bigger ones.

Ponzu sauce is a Japanese yuzu-flavored soy sauce that has the most refreshing taste. You can find it next to the soy sauce in Japanese grocery stores. If you don't have it, add a bit of lime juice to regular soy sauce.

If the whole roll adventure is more hassle than fun to you, try doing this as a salad by increasing the amount of rice vermicelli a little.

SERVES 2 AS A LIGHT MEAL (MAKES 8 MEDIUM ROLLS)
PREPPING TIME 30 MINUTES   COOKING TIME 2 MINUTES

GAZPACHO WITH ZUCCHINI AND SAGE BRIWATS

INGREDIENTS

FOR THE GAZPACHO

14 oz. (400 g) fresh ripe
    tomatoes, roughly
    diced
1 small red bell pepper,
    deseeded and roughly
    diced
1 small garlic clove,
    grated
1 small peperoncino,
    crushed
salt, pepper
a drizzle of olive oil
a few torn basil leaves

FOR THE BRIWATS
(MAKES 8)

1 small zucchini
6 tbsp. olive oil
a dozen sage leaves,
    chopped
4 oz. (115 g) fresh
    brousse or ricotta
1 garlic clove, grated
½ tsp. lemon zest
4 brick pastry circles
    (12 in./30 cm wide)

In the sizzling days of summer, it feels like one dinner out of two ends up being a gazpacho. Not much can compete with it: it allows the pure taste of the tomatoes to shine, it's refreshing, requires no cooking, and is put together in minutes. It's a pure seasonal treat, something you can and want to make only at that precise moment in time. The variation that I prefer involves sweet red bell pepper, which brings a velvety texture and an enticing reddish-pink color to it.

I like to balance the freshness of the gazpacho by pairing it with something salty, dense, and crunchy. On most days, Manchego on rustic bread is enough, but when I can muster a bit of courage, I cook these crunchy brick dumplings. The idea of making briwats comes from Morocco (similar brick dumplings exist all over the Middle East), but the filling here is more Italian inspired.

First make the gazpacho. In a large mixing bowl, use a hand blender to blend the tomatoes, bell pepper, garlic, and peperoncino until smooth. Salt and pepper to taste. Wait until serving to add the olive oil and basil. Put the bowl in the fridge while you prepare the briwats.

Grate the zucchini in a strainer, add two pinches of salt, and leave it to drain for a few minutes.

Heat up 2 tablespoons of olive oil in a non-stick pan (the same you'll use to fry the briwats) and fry the sage leaves for a few minutes, until slightly golden and crispy. Put in a bowl to stop the cooking while you prepare the rest. Don't wash the pan, you'll use it later.

Press the zucchini in the strainer to remove as much liquid as you can. Transfer to a mixing bowl with the brousse, garlic, lemon zest, and black pepper. Mix well with a fork.

Cut your brick circles in half with a pair of scissors. Put a small tablespoon of the brousse mix in one corner and fold the circle over itself to form a triangular dumpling. Put it on a plate and make the 7 others in the same way.

Heat up your pan on high heat, add the remaining 4 tablespoons of olive oil and quickly put your briwats to fry (watch out for the hot oil). Wait until they're light brown before flipping them. Fry them for 3–4 minutes on each side, lowering the heat if they color too fast.

Once ready, drain on paper towels before dividing them between two small serving plates. Pour the gazpacho into bowls, top with a drizzle of olive oil and a few torn basil leaves.

As a rule, I try to keep tomatoes out of the fridge, but in this case, putting them in the fridge a few hours beforehand will ensure your gazpacho is cold right away. If you haven't planned ahead, you can drop a few ice cubes into it before serving—just don't wait too long before eating! The classic method would be to do the gazpacho ahead of time and then put it in the fridge, but I feel too much planning ahead goes against the carefree nature of a good summer meal.

Pick a small, fresh zucchini for this. Bigger ones will tend to have more seeds and be more watery.

Folding the brick pastry in triangles is relatively easy, but if you don't do it often it's perfectly normal that the first ones turn out a bit wonky. The good news is that no matter how imperfect, they will still taste good. Don't put in too much filling and you'll be fine.

SERVES 2 AS A LIGHT MEAL
COOKING TIME 10 MINUTES

NECTARINE AND
TOMATO PANZANELLA

INGREDIENTS

9 tbsp. olive oil
2 slices of sourdough
    bread or ciabatta, cut
    in ¾ in. (2 cm) chunks
1½ oz. (40 g) whole
    almonds,
    cut lengthwise
1 tbsp. fennel seeds
1 small garlic clove,
    grated
18½ oz. (525 g) heirloom
    tomatoes, cut in
    quarters
8¼ oz. (235 g) white
    nectarines, cut in
    ½ in. (1 cm)-wide slices
a handful of basil leaves,
    torn
1 mozzarella di bufala ball
    (9 oz./250 g),
    torn roughly
salt, pepper

This particular combination is the essence of summer carefree abundance to me. It's rich, juicy, and a bit frivolous in the way that half of its ingredients could belong in a dessert. It's ridiculously simple to put together and yet it can only be done at this time of year, which to my mind makes it more of a luxury than anything. To really shine, it requires a bit of effort on the ingredient side: great tomatoes, nectarines, mozzarella, and a powerful, green olive oil are a must.

Heat up 4 tablespoons of olive oil in a non-stick pan, add the bread followed by the almonds, fennel seeds, and a bit of pepper. Leave to cook for a few minutes until the bread is golden and crispy on the edges.

Meanwhile, put 5 tablespoons of olive oil in a mixing bowl along with the garlic. Mix well, then add the tomatoes, nectarines, and basil. Season to taste and mix again before adding the croutons and mozzarella. Mix gently and serve in bowls.

This is obviously a great way to use stale bread.

The firm texture of a nectarine will hold better than a peach for this. White varieties have a more delicate taste than yellow ones. If you can find them, blood nectarines would also work nicely.

For optimum taste, the tomatoes and nectarines should not be cold. Keep them at room temperature for a few days or, even better, keep them out of the fridge altogether. Don't hesitate to mix tomato varieties, playing with the color and tastes of yellow, black, green, red, or pink tomatoes.

This one can sit a little at room temperature before serving for flavours to develop, if you don't mind the bread getting a bit softer.

SERVES 2 AS A LIGHT MEAL
COOKING TIME   5 MINUTES

THE SIMPLEST FARE CERTAINLY TASTES
BETTER WITH A SIDE OF FRESH
AIR AND DRAMATIC VIEWS. IT MAKES
WHATEVER WAS SOUGHT OUT OR FORAGED
FOR THE OCCASION ALL THE MORE
EXCEPTIONAL. SOMETIMES IT'S ALL I NEED
TO GET EXCITED ABOUT FOOD AGAIN.

1   A simple tomato, pomegranate, and fresh herb salad becomes luxury when eaten on the rocky floor of the garrigue.

2   My passion for picnics was probably prompted by a trip to the Azores islands where the abundance of scenic spots makes you want to completely forgo indoor dining.

3   Even a modest cheese platter turns into luxury when you're in the wild.

WATERMELON CARPACCIO
WITH RED CURRANTS

INGREDIENTS

FOR THE CARPACCIO

16 oz. (450 g) watermelon,
   cut in 2 in. (5 cm)
   triangles
a handful of red currants,
   stems removed
¾ oz. (25 g) rucola
¾ oz. (25 g) fresh
   coriander leaves
2 oz. (60 g) feta
salt, pepper

FOR THE DRESSING

6 tbsp. olive oil
2 tsp. light liquid honey
   such as lavender
   or lime tree
2 level tsp. 'nduja

My grandparents used to have a whole hedge of currants, which in my kid's mind was a complete loss of space when they could have had more exciting—namely sweeter—berries in their place. How I miss that hedge now! Currants here can be found in tiny and pricy containers at the supermarket, but the real bounty lies in people's gardens. They're the kind of berries you'll find by chance on a small stall at the market, the kind your neighbors might give you because they're not using them. They're pretty elusive and when I finally score a bunch of them I proceed to put them on everything for a week. Like pomegranate seeds, they have a gently sour quality that does wonders in savory dishes.

Here, they're fancying up a watermelon and feta salad and turning it into a beautiful carpaccio. I always feel like I need to balance watermelon's tendency toward blandness. With the help of rucola, coriander, and 'nduja, this plate walks an interesting line between spicy and refreshing.

Lay the watermelon slices on two flat plates. Add the red currants, rucola, coriander, and crumbled feta on top. Add salt and pepper to taste.

In a separate bowl, mix the dressing ingredients. When ready to serve, drizzle the dressing over each plate.

If you can't find 'nduja, you can try using another spicy paste.

SERVES 2 AS A LIGHT MEAL
PREPARATION TIME 10 MINUTES

ZA'ATAR MAN'OUCHE WITH
MOUTABAL, LABNEH, AND TOMATOES

INGREDIENTS

4½ oz. (125 g) all-purpose
    flour
½ tsp. fine salt
1 tbsp. olive oil
5½ tbsp. (80 ml) warm
    water
1½ tsp. (5 g) fresh yeast
1 level tsp. unrefined
    sugar

FOR THE MOUTABAL

8 tbsp. olive oil
1 small eggplant, cut in
    ½ in. (1 cm) slices
1 small garlic clove,
    grated
3 tbsp. lemon juice
1 level tbsp. whole tahini
salt, pepper

FOR THE LABNEH

3 tbsp. Greek yogurt

FOR THE ZA'ATAR

5 tbsp. dried oregano
3 tbsp. golden roasted
    sesame seeds
3 tbsp.
    coriander seeds,
    crushed
2 tsp. sumac powder
½ tsp. fleur de sel
5 tbsp. olive oil

FOR THE TOMATOES

1 heirloom tomato, cut
    in ½ in. (1 cm) dice
1 spring onion, finely
    chopped
a few coriander sprigs
4 tbsp. olive oil
salt, pepper

I grew up with a baguette on the table at every meal. When I discovered flatbread, I was somehow relieved that the cliché was wrong and that French bread wasn't the only one worth eating. I discovered man'ouches on a trip to Beirut, where they're eaten for breakfast. I even ate them with labneh and jam at some point of the trip but have since returned to more conservative French ways and now rather have them as lunch.

The core of the recipe is the man'ouche paired with labneh, but I like to make a more balanced meal by pairing it with vegetables—here a moutabal and tomato salad.

Two hours before serving, prepare the man'ouche dough. Mix the flour and salt in a mixing bowl. In a smaller bowl, mix the olive oil, warm water, yeast, and sugar. Stir with a spoon until the yeast is dissolved. Make a well in the flour and put the liquid mix at the center. Mix with a fork and then with your hands to form a ball. Knead for a few minutes until smooth and no longer sticky. Put back in the bowl, cover with plastic wrap, and leave to rest in a warm room for 2 hours.

Meanwhile, cook the eggplant for the moutabal so it has time to cool down. Heat 6 tablespoons of olive oil in a non-stick plan. Lay the eggplant slices in the pan, avoiding any overlap. Add salt and pepper, cover, and cook on medium-high heat for 7 minutes on each side. They should be soft and slightly browned. Add more oil and lower the heat if they start to stick. Once done, transfer to a plate and allow to cool at room temperature before putting in the fridge.

To prepare the labneh put the yogurt at the center of a fine, clean dish towel. For such a small quantity I use an old towel that's been cut in four. Form a pouch with the towel, pressing the liquid out of the yogurt through the fabric. Get as much as you can out before putting the pouch in a strainer and bowl. Leave it in the fridge until serving.

Mix all the za'atar ingredients in a bowl and leave at room temperature until using.

Right before eating, finish the moutabal by mixing all the ingredients in a food processor until you get a smooth texture.

Prepare the tomato salad before starting to cook the man'ouches and leave it at room temperature.

To cook the man'ouches, heat up a pan on high heat. Divide your dough into balls 4 equal-sized and spread them as you go in 8 in. (20 cm)-wide circles. As you put each of them in the pan, spread a quarter of the za'atar on top before folding it on itself. Cook for 2 minutes. They should color only slightly and remain soft.

Assemble the tomatoes, moutabal, and labneh in a bowl, top with a bit of extra olive oil, and serve with the man'ouches on the side.

Labneh can be found in Middle Eastern stores, saving you the straining part. If you can find really thick Greek yogurt you can also skip this step.

You can also substitute thyme for oregano.

Using white or zebra eggplants, whose skins are more tender, saves you from peeling them.

Fresh yeast can be replaced by dry yeast. In that case, divide the quantities by 2.

SERVES 2 AS A MAIN
RESTING TIME 2 HOURS   COOKING TIME 20 MINUTES FOR THE MAN'OUCHE

HEAVY WITH DUST AND PERFUME, A MELANCHOLIC
SLICE OF SUMMER SET IN THE VANISHING
GRANDEUR OF LEBANON. IN THE CRUMBLING
FAÇADES OF BEIRUT MANSIONS, AND IN
THE ROMAN RUINS OF TYRE AND BAALBEK
EVERYTHING IS PRECIOUS AND FLEETING.

1   On the terrace of an old Beirut apartment, fresh lemonade offers respite from the heat and chaos.

2   Late afternoon on Tyre's seaside, right by the ruins of the ancient city.

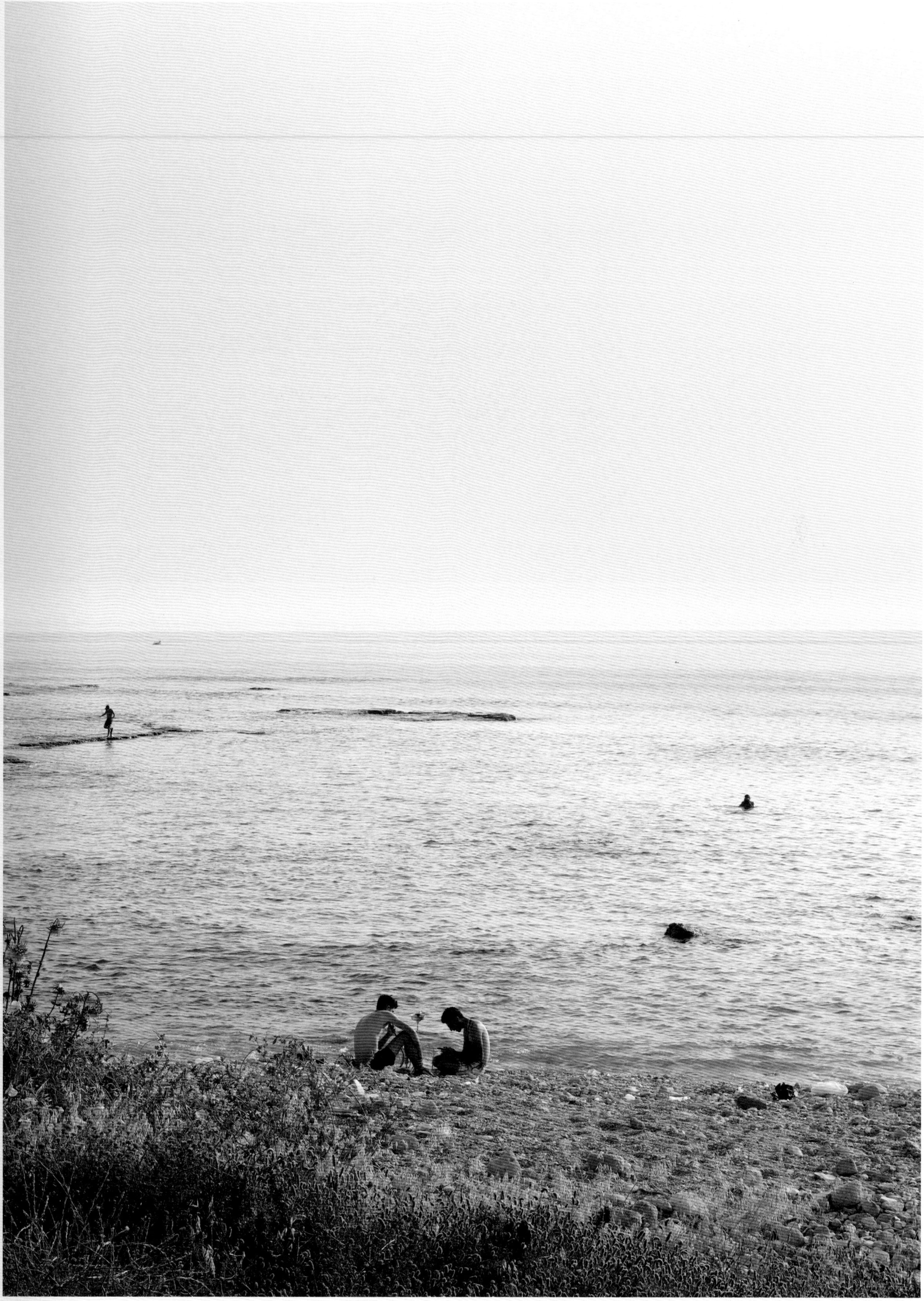

SUMMER
SAFFRON RICE

INGREDIENTS

FOR THE RICE

5½ oz. (160 g) white
    basmati rice, soaked
    for 30 minutes
1 tbsp. olive oil, plus
    extra to drizzle
salt
1 tomato, diced
a few coriander sprigs,
    chopped
1 lime (optional)

FOR THE SAUCE

1 tsp. saffron threads
2 tbsp. boiling water
3 tbsp. thick Greek yogurt
3 tbsp. olive oil
salt, pepper

FOR THE ONIONS

1 red onion, cut in
    ⅛ in. (½ cm) slices
1 tbsp. almonds,
    halved lengthwise
1 tbsp. fennel seeds
1 tsp. black mustard seeds
5 tbsp. olive oil

My first memorable experience with rice must go back to the first time I went to India. Before that, I confess that rice felt like a bland side, a poor challenger to enticing Italian pasta. I went to India wondering if my body would be able to handle its food, and instead I put on a few pounds, mostly thanks to the irresistible mountains of delicate and fragrant rice that accompanied almost every meal. Appreciation for all kinds of other rice followed, but my first love was long-grain basmati rice. This recipe is somewhere between a salad, a biryani, and a tahdig. It requires minimum cooking for a rich result—a great asset when the heat rises. It makes good use of our local saffron and provides a refreshing update to our summer staples: tomatoes and olive oil.

Put your rice in a bowl to soak.

Pre-heat your oven to 400 °F (200 °C).

For the sauce, grind your saffron threads to a powder in a mortar. Add the boiling water, mix, and leave aside while you prepare the rest.
For the onions, lay your red onion slices in an oven tray, top with the almonds, and the fennel and mustard seeds. Drizzle with the olive oil. Add a good pinch of salt and a bit of pepper. Cook in the oven for 12 minutes, until the onions start to get dark brown and crispy.

Meanwhile, drain the uncooked rice and put it in a hot saucepan with a tablespoon of olive oil. Mix to coat the grains and add one and a half times the rice volume in water (twice the volume if unsoaked). Add a pinch of coarse salt to the water. Cover and cook on high heat for 4 minutes, lowering to medium for 4 more minutes. Remember that soaked rice cooks quicker.

Once the rice is ready (the grains should retain a slight bite and not stick to one another), switch off the heat and keep the lid on until serving.

While the rice cooks, finish the sauce by adding the saffron water to a small bowl with the yogurt, olive oil, a good pinch of salt, and a bit of pepper.

When the onions are cooked, transfer them to the rice pan, keeping a few to garnish. Carefully fold the onions into the rice with a wooden spoon. Divide the rice between two large bowls, spoon the saffron sauce on one side, add the diced tomatoes, remaining onions, and fresh coriander. Add a pinch of salt and a drizzle of olive oil to the tomatoes.

Serve with lime quarters if you like.

It's always better to soak the rice if you have time, even for 10 minutes. If you can't, just rinse it until the water runs clear.

Be sure to salt every component properly.

You can replace the tomato with cucumber, or even mix the two.

SERVES 2 AS A MAIN
COOKING TIME   15 MINUTES   SOAKING TIME   30 MINUTES

2

AS THE LANDSCAPE TURNS GOLDEN AT THE
MERCY OF HIGH-SUMMER HEAT BURSTS,
ONE LEARNS TO SEE BEAUTY IN THESE DRIED
STALKS. THEY ANNOUNCE THE HARVEST,
CAN INSPIRE A WHOLE VOCABULARY OF
BASKETRY, AND PAIR WELL WITH ANOTHER
POOR-MAN'S GOLD: BRASS.

1　Trivets, mortars, and baskets—three things one can't ever have enough of.

2　A dried wild artichoke flower, leaving no doubt about its thistle kinship.

GRAPEFRUIT AND MARZIPAN ICE CREAM
WITH SALTED CARAMEL ALMONDS

INGREDIENTS

FOR THE ICE CREAM

1 pink grapefruit
3½ oz. (100 g) organic
    unflavored marzipan,
    diced
⅓ cup (90 ml) cold
    unsweetened
    almond milk
3 tbsp. agave syrup

FOR THE SALTED
CARAMEL ALMONDS

1 oz. (25 g) coconut
    or unrefined sugar
½ oz. (15 g) butter
3 pinches of fleur de sel
3 oz. (80 g) almonds

Investing in a good ice-cream maker the first summer we moved to Provence felt a bit frivolous. Would summer last that long? Would the fruits be that plentiful? Yes, on both counts. But more importantly, ice-cream making turned out to be a pretty easy affair if you followed your instincts and it freed me from over-sweetened and overpriced preparations. Homemade ice creams tend to grow hard once refrozen, so it's best to make it right before you eat. The ice-cream mixture can be made in advance, though, and it's even advisable to make it the day before to allow flavors to develop. But don't lose the carefree pleasure of ice cream with too much planning ahead. This should remain an easygoing treat.

In the summer, we get beautiful pink grapefruits from Corsica that make the most delicate sherbet. Topped with caramelized almonds, this has a very satisfying mix of sweet, salty, and tangy.

Put water to boil in a saucepan. With a peeler, remove the zest from the grapefruit and set aside. With a knife, discard most of the white pith underneath. Cut the fruit in half and put it with the zest to boil for 5 minutes. Drain and allow to cool before transferring it to the fridge. You want it to be cold before using.

Blitz the grapefruit, its zest, the marzipan, and almond milk with a hand blender until smooth. Taste the mixture before adding the agave syrup. Depending on how sweet the other ingredients are, you might not even need it. My rule of thumb is that the flavor should be slightly sweeter than you'd like for the frozen result to be good.

Transfer the mixture to the ice-cream machine and churn according to the maker's instructions.

Meanwhile, prepare the salted caramel almonds (this can also be done ahead of time). Put the sugar, butter, and a pinch of fleur de sel in a saucepan on medium heat. Mix for a couple of minutes until it forms a smooth sauce. Add the almonds and stir well to coat them before turning up the heat until it starts to bubble and slightly darken. Remove from heat as soon as it slightly darkens—caramel burns quickly! Spread on parchment paper, add a pinch of fleur de sel, and let it cool down. When ready to serve, top the ice cream with a few almonds and another pinch of fleur de sel.

The taste of almond milk varies wildly depending on brand. To cook and to drink, I favor the ones with the more intense taste and thicker texture.

This will make more caramel almonds than needed. The ones that remain will be a nice snack to have around or to scatter on Greek yogurt.

If you don't own an ice-cream maker, you can also turn the mix into popsicles by simply freezing it.

SERVES 4 SCOOPS
COOKING TIME 5 MINUTES   COOL-DOWN TIME 2 HOURS
CHURNING TIME 40 MINUTES (DEPENDING ON THE MACHINE)

I LOVE IT WHEN CAREFULLY ARRANGED
PRODUCTS GIVE WAY TO PILES
AND MOUNTAINS, WHEN FLOWERS AND
VEGETABLES COLLIDE, AND IMPROVISATION
IS ITS OWN KIND OF BEAUTY. THAT'S
WHAT YOU GET IN THE FEVERISH ABUNDANCE
OF SUMMER MARKETS.

1   Bread sold outside on market day in the neighboring town of Nyons.
2   The impossibly vibrant Sighişoara market in Romania and its impressive melon section.

EARLY

FALL

This is one bittersweet transition. As fall starts to loom, I'm usually torn between looking with anguish at what betrays a dimming summer and seeing it as the slow-burning fire it has become, with much left to give. Nonetheless, farewells are in the air. Each swim feels like the last and summer produce is dwindling.

It's the final hurrah for tomatoes, more abundant, ripe, and affordable than ever. I'm past the deference granted to first specimens and just think about thick, lavish sauces when I see them. I tell myself I'll make jars for the cold season but always eat half the stash before temperatures drop.

Winter feels like a distant thing as my fridge and counter overflows with the joint parade of summer and fall goods. The much-awaited figs and pomegranates finally arrive while eggplants become the season's favorite for their comforting yet summery taste. I'm back to creating slightly more elaborate dishes, ones that take longer to cook and have the deeper taste I'm craving again.

GRILLED FIG
AND ZUCCHINI SALAD

INGREDIENTS

8½ oz. (240 g) zucchini
1 tbsp. white balsamic
    vinegar
8 tbsp. olive oil
7 oz. (200 g) fresh black
    figs, quartered
3½ oz. (100 g) stale
    bread, roughly cut
    in chunks
1 garlic clove, crushed
¾ oz. (20 g) hazelnuts,
    halved
3½ oz. (100 g) mozzarella
    di bufala
2 tbsp. young savory
    leaves
salt, pepper

Figs are one of those fruits that travel easily between sweet and savory dishes. My absolute favorite thing is to eat them with ricotta and chestnut honey, but I'll happily throw them in salads too. This recipe really sits between summer and fall. It's still refreshing while dabbling with the deeper taste of roasted fruits that will be a staple of the colder months. I like that it's quick to assemble while feeling pretty sophisticated.

Slice your zucchini into ribbons with a mandoline on the thinnest setting. Lay them on a flat plate, drizzle with the vinegar, 2 tablespoons of olive oil, 2 pinches of salt, and a grind of black pepper. Mix gently to coat and leave to rest at room temperature while you prepare the rest.

Heat 2 tablespoons of olive oil in a non-stick pan. Set the figs in along with salt and pepper and let them cook for a few minutes on very high heat. You want them to color without breaking. Put aside on a plate once done. Don't wash the pan, you'll use it for the breadcrumbs.

Use an electric mixer to turn your stale bread into medium-sized crumbs. Put them in your pan along with the remaining 4 tablespoons of olive oil, crushed garlic, hazelnuts, salt, and pepper. Mix well and cook on high heat for 3–5 minutes, until light brown and crispy. Turn off the heat and start assembling the plates.

Start with the zucchini strips, then use a pair of tongs to place the figs, spread over the torn pieces of mozzarella, scatter over the breadcrumbs and the savory leaves, and finish with a drizzle of good olive oil.

Like all raw zucchini recipes, this calls for a very firm and fresh zucchini.

If you can't find figs, this also works great with white nectarines.

SERVES 2 AS A LIGHT MEAL
COOKING TIME 5–10 MINUTES

MULTIGRAIN
GALETTES

INGREDIENTS

FOR THE
TOMATO SAUCE

3 tbsp. olive oil
1 big garlic clove, crushed
1 tbsp. harissa paste
1 lb. 5 oz. (600 g) ripe
   tomatoes, grated
1 tbsp. unrefined sugar
salt, pepper

FOR THE GALETTES

4½ oz. (130 g) mixed
   quinoa
salt
1 egg
2 tbsp. sesame seeds
2 tbsp. kasha
1 tbsp. coriander seeds
1¼ oz. (35 g) Emmental,
   grated
3 tbsp. olive oil

6¼ oz. (180 g) zucchini,
   cut in ½ in.
   (1 cm)-wide sticks
2 tbsp. olive oil
1 big garlic clove, crushed
salt, pepper

To my mind, the quick way to comfort food involves tomato sauce. In order not to have spaghetti al pomodoro every other day, I do make an effort to switch things up a bit. I cook galettes with many kinds of cereals, but quinoa is the one that really shines, with its airy and crunchy texture. If quinoa sounds like a healthy punishment, I offer this recipe as an attempt to change your mind. A bit of cheese helps make it more transgressive, but really it's the great balance between something reassuring yet very flavorful that takes it home for me.

Start with the tomato sauce. Heat up the olive oil in a saucepan, add the garlic and harissa, and wait a couple of minutes before adding the tomatoes, sugar, salt, and pepper. Mix with a wooden spoon and leave to simmer uncovered for 15 minutes.

Meanwhile, rinse and strain your quinoa and cook in another saucepan, covered by one and a half times its volume in cold water. Bring to a boil then lower the heat to medium, cover, and cook for 10 minutes, until the water has been absorbed and it's still a bit crunchy. Add salt only toward the end of the cooking.

While the quinoa cooks, beat the egg with a fork in a mixing bowl and add the sesame seeds, kasha, coriander seeds, and cheese. Pour in the warm quinoa (heat it up if it's cold) and mix well.

Heat up 3 tablespoons of the olive oil in a non-stick flat pan. Drop tablespoons of the galette mixture into the hot pan, spreading them slightly with the back of the spoon. Don't worry about making them perfectly round, but don't make them too big or they will be difficult to flip. Cook on high heat until crispy and brown and easy to flip, around 5 minutes on each side.

Roughly at the same time, in another pan, put your zucchini to cook on medium-high heat with the olive oil and the garlic. Add salt and pepper and cook until slightly colored and a bit soft.

When ready to eat, spread the tomato sauce in two shallow plates, arrange the galettes on top, and finish with the zucchini.

Don't bother grating your tomatoes if you can find some of the San Marzano variety. These almost turn to sauce the minute you put them in the pan. You can also use a bottle of polpa di pomodoro if tomato season is already over.

This recipe can be made with regular quinoa or only black or red, but I think the mixed variety has more visual appeal.

Kasha is roasted buckwheat. Here it brings a bit of crunch and depth to the galettes.

Remember that you don't need to cook everything at the same time. Start with the tomato sauce and quinoa, and once they're done, cook the galettes and zucchini.

This is also a great way to use up leftover cooked quinoa.

SERVES 2 AS A MAIN
COOKING TIME   30 MINUTES

YIAHNI,
A GREEK POTATO STEW

INGREDIENTS

8 tbsp. olive oil
2 garlic cloves, chopped
2 tbsp. dried oregano
1 dried peperoncino,
   crushed
2 tbsp. paprika powder
15 oz. (420 g) white or
   zebra eggplants
   cut in ¾ in. (2 cm) dices
salt, pepper
1½ lb. (670 g) ripe
   tomatoes, diced
1 big tbsp.
   capers in vinegar,
   drained
17½ oz. (500 g) waxy
   potatoes, quartered
2¾ oz. (80 g) feta to serve

A few years ago, I spent a week on the Greek island of Tinos in October. The tourist season had come to an end and on the now-deserted island the weather was playing a game of hot and cold with us, offering baths in a still-warm sea on some days and sweeping us off our feet with fierce meltemi winds on others. This made me crave a combination of summer lunches and fall dinners. At the tiny local market on the harbor, the last tomatoes and eggplants were sitting among piles of homemade preserves: capers, dried tomatoes, olives ... Potatoes sounded like a comforting option and ended up in the same pot as I was cooking with the moonlit sea in sight. I later found out that this kind of stew was called yiahni.
This particular version evokes a fall nurtured by the summer that has just passed, one that retains some of its warmth and richness.

Heat up the olive oil in a deep, non-stick skillet. Add the garlic, oregano, peperoncino, and paprika and leave to color on medium-high heat for a minute or so. Add the eggplant and stir well to coat them with the oil. Add salt and pepper, cover, and leave to cook for 5 minutes.

Add the tomatoes, capers, and potatoes. Lower the heat to medium, cover again, and leave to cook for 50 minutes, checking regularly. Once done, you should be able to slide a knife easily through the potatoes and they should have an amber-ish color. Taste for salt but remember the feta will add extra saltiness.

When ready to eat, divide between two large bowls and top with the crumbled feta. Finish with a bit of good olive oil.

Fresh tomatoes can be replaced by canned tomatoes. In which case, feel free to add a couple of sun-dried tomatoes for a deeper taste and a bit of sugar to balance acidity.

Like any stew, this one welcomes variations. A favorite of mine is to switch capers for black olives and eggplants for a mix of bell peppers and sweet onions.

TATIN
ALLA NORMA

INGREDIENTS
FOR THE TATIN

5 tbsp. olive oil
1 level tbsp. honey
1 large white or zebra
    eggplant, cut in ⅔ in.
    (1½ cm) slices
2 large fleshy tomatoes,
    cut in ⅔ in. (1½ cm)
    slices, deseeded
salt, pepper
a few basil leaves,
    to serve
2 tbsp. fresh ricotta,
    crumbled, to serve

FOR THE CRUST

3 oz. (80 g) all-purpose
    flour
1½ oz. (45 g) fine
    semolina flour, plus
    more for dusting
3 oz. (80 g) einkorn
    flour
½ tsp. salt
6 tbsp. water
4 tbsp. olive oil

As tomato season comes to an end, gone is the respect for the first beautiful specimens that commanded you eat them raw with barely more than olive oil and salt. At this point of the year, huge ripe tomatoes sit on my counter and beg to be transformed into something sweeter still.

The tomato pies of my childhood often led to soggy disappointments. This recipe is an act of revenge on all of those. It uses the idea of the French tatin (an upside-down pie) to get the best of both worlds: browned, almost confit vegetables sitting on a flaky crust. It's also inspired by the classic Italian recipe of pasta alla norma, an eggplant and tomato sauce topped with ricotta salata.

Heat the olive oil and honey in your tatin pan, then lay your eggplant slices over the base in a single layer with minimum overlap. Add salt and pepper, cover, and cook on high heat for 5 minutes, until they have browned on one side. Carefully flip them with a pair of tongs, still avoiding overlaps, and add some extra oil if it looks a bit dry.

Layer the tomatoes on top, add salt and pepper, cover again, and cook on high heat for 5 minutes. Lower to medium heat, remove the lid, and leave to cook for 30 minutes, until most of the juices have evaporated.

Prepare the crust while the vegetables are cooking. Mix the flours and the salt in a bowl, form a well, pour in the water and oil and mix gently with a fork until a ball forms. Don't knead the dough. Cover and leave in the fridge until the eggplants and tomatoes are ready.

Pre-heat your oven to 400 °F (200 °C). Turn off the heat of the vegetables. On a lightly floured surface, roll out your dough with a rolling pin into a circle slightly larger than your pan. Carefully wrap your dough on the pin to transfer to the pan. Gently press unroll the dough and press it down into the sides of the pan and poke a dozen holes in the dough with a knife. Bake in the oven for 35 minutes.

When the pie is cooked, carefully flip it out onto a round platter. A couple of eggplant slices might stay at the bottom of the pan, use a pair of tongs to put them back in place. Top with small chunks of ricotta, basil leaves, and a splash of good olive oil.

When it comes to eggplant, the zebra and white varieties are my first choice for their tender skin and sweeter taste.

My favorite kind of ricotta is ricotta di pecora (made from sheep's milk). If you don't have ricotta, mozzarella di bufala or ricotta salata are also great on top.

Semolina flour is made from hard durum wheat and gives a pleasant crunchy and bread-like taste to dishes. It's easily found in Italian stores.

FOR A 12 IN. (30 CM)-DIAMETER NON-STICK PAN
THAT CAN GO FROM THE STOVE TO THE OVEN
SERVES 4 AS A LIGHT MEAL, 2 AS A MAIN
COOKING TIME 1 HOUR AND 10 MINUTES

ONE WAY TO PREPARE FOR THE RIGORS OF
WINTER IS TO SPEND A FEW OCTOBER
DAYS ON TINOS IN GREECE. IT IS A PILGRIMAGE
OF SORTS, A COCKTAIL OF SEA, SUN,
AND ROCK SO POWERFUL IT STRENGTHENS
YOU FOR THE MONTHS TO COME.

1   Barren yet beautiful, the landscape is a testament to resilience.

2   On days where the meltemi is kind enough to stop blowing, a rejuvenating swim in the sapphire waters.

3   Crowded with Orthodox pilgrims in the summer, the island is blissfully empty in the fall.

EGGPLANT AND
HALLOUMI BOWL

INGREDIENTS

10 tbsp. olive oil
1 medium-sized sweet
    onion, cut in ½ in.
    (1 cm) slices
2 tsp. Aleppo pepper
2 tsp. ground coriander
14 oz. (400 g) white
    or zebra eggplants,
    cut lengthwise in
    2½ × ½ in. (6 × 1 cm)
    slices
4½ oz. (130 g) tomatoes,
    diced
6 oz. (170 g) pomegranate
    seeds
7 oz. (200 g) halloumi
    cheese, cut in ½ in.
    (1 cm) slices
juice of half a lemon
1 garlic clove, grated
salt, pepper
a small bouquet of
    fresh coriander
a few flatbreads, to serve
    (for a homemade
    version see
    the man'ouche
    recipe p. 128, just
    hold the za'atar)

I remember the first night I tasted halloumi like others remember their first kiss. It was in a candlelit, 16th-century Andalusian courtyard, so I'd venture to say it was also more romantic than most first kisses. I didn't even know of its existence before that blessed evening, which made the discovery all the more delightful. In a single blow it made a compelling case for skipping meat and ruined a probably much more reasonable tofu alternative (it would take me years to reconsider). As the Cyprus cheese got more fashionable it also became easier to find, opening the possibility of cooking it at home.

Here, its salty taste and thick texture plays well with the softness of eggplant and benefits from the tangy kick of pomegranate and tomatoes.

Heat up 4 tablespoons of the olive oil in a non-stick pan, add the onion, Aleppo pepper, and ground coriander. Stir with a spatula and leave to cook on medium heat for 3–5 minutes before adding the eggplant. Add 4 more tablespoons of olive oil, salt, and pepper. Stir, cover, and leave to cook for 15 minutes on medium-high heat. Check regularly and add more olive oil if it sticks. The eggplant should be light brown and soft.

Meanwhile, put your tomatoes and pomegranate seeds in a bowl, season with salt, pepper, and 2 tablespoons of olive oil. Leave at room temperature until serving.

When your eggplant and onions are halfway done, heat up a flat plan on high heat to cook the halloumi. Lay the slices on the hot pan, no oil needed. Depending on the cheese, it will take a few minutes on each side. Cook until well browned.

Turn off the heat on both pans. Mix the lemon juice and grated garlic into the eggplant with a wooden spoon.

Assemble the ingredients in a bowl, starting with the eggplant followed by the tomatoes and pomegranate, the halloumi slices, and a good bunch of chopped fresh coriander. Serve with flatbread on the side.

This recipe also works well with either only tomatoes or only pomegranate seeds.

Feel free to roll this into a flatbread for a decadent, albeit probably messy, sandwich.

SERVES 2 AS A MAIN
COOKING TIME 25 MINUTES

TIAN DE
COURGETTES

INGREDIENTS

4 tbsp. olive oil
2 garlic cloves,
    crushed
half a dried peperoncino,
    crushed
1 lb. 2 oz. (500 g) zucchini,
    cut in ⅕ in. (½ cm)
    slices
1 small preserved
    lemon, rinsed and
    chopped thinly
1 tsp. dried oregano
1½ oz. (45 g) white
    basmati rice
2 eggs
5½ tbsp. heavy cream
1⅖ oz. (40 g) Parmigiano-
    Reggiano, grated
2 tbsp. capers in
    vinegar, drained
3 tbsp. pine nuts
salt, pepper

A tian is a rather loose designation for a dish from Provence that is generally made of summer vegetables roasted in the oven. Because of its ancient origin and its dialect-style name, it brings images of medieval Provence to my mind. The Middle Ages felt like an extremely distant time when I was living in Paris, where the idea of the past revolved mostly around 19th-century history. Here in the countryside it's very different; we live among Roman chapels, walk centuries-old paths, and find castle ruins hidden in the maquis. It's a much lighter, romantic, and pastoral vision of medieval times, at odds with the gothic cathedrals of my youth, and it makes your imagination wander. I'm inspired by cooking ideas that endured through centuries—that out of the same land, the same products, you can still find pleasure in the same associations. It's the thrill of eating figs with fresh ricotta and honey like it's 500 BCE, or the pleasure of cooking a tian as they've been doing here for longer than I can imagine.
In this variation, the rather rustic canvas of zucchini, rice, and eggs gains sophistication by fragrant seasoning and cooked in a thin crispy layer.

Heat the olive oil on high heat in a non-stick pan. Add the garlic cloves and peperoncino, followed a minute later by the zucchini, lemon, and oregano. Mix to coat and leave to cook for 2–3 minutes, until the zucchini starts to color. Do not add salt yet.

Meanwhile, rinse your rice until the water runs clear. Drain and add to the zucchini. Mix and cook with a lid on medium-low heat for 25 minutes. When ready, add some pepper and taste to check if it needs salt. Remember the parmigiano and capers in the batter will add some extra saltiness.

Once ready, pre-heat your oven to 350 °F (180 °C). In a mixing bowl beat the eggs with a fork before adding the cream and parmigiano. Keep a bit of parmigiano to spread on top. Add the zucchini-rice mix and the capers, mixing carefully. Transfer to an 8 × 11 in. (20 × 28 cm) oven dish, spread the pine nuts and remaining parmigiano on top, and bake in the oven for 30 minutes, until brown and crispy on top.

Serve hot or at room temperature with a simple tomato salad. To bring an acidic touch, I like to season the tomatoes with a mix of olive oil and lemon juice or olive oil and pomegranate syrup.

Look for jars of preserved lemons in Middle Eastern stores. They keep for a long time. They are also fairly easy to make if you can't find any to buy.

Good-quality capers make a huge difference. The vinegar ones are better for cooking, while I prefer their olive oil counterpart for eating as is.

This tastes great when reheated, so don't hesitate to double the quantities. I think it's better when not too thick, so consider using a wider dish to cook it.

The concept of this recipe can be adapted to other summer vegetables, but zucchini is my favorite.

SERVES 2 AS A MAIN
COOKING TIME 55 MINUTES

LEMON, ALMOND, AND POLENTA CAKE

INGREDIENTS

4¼ oz. (120 g) coconut
    oil, softened,
    plus extra to grease
4 oz. (100 g) golden sugar
zest of 1 lemon,
    grated juice of 1 lemon
¼ tsp. vanilla extract
6¼ oz. (180 g) ground
    almonds
2½ oz. (70 g) pre-cooked
    polenta
1¼ oz. (35 g) rice flour
1 tsp. baking powder
a pinch of salt
2 eggs, beaten
a handful of blackberries

There's a bit of southern Italy in this association, even more with the generous amount of almonds involved. I like to have a few recipes of quickly thrown together cakes for when the weather is taking a turn and you suddenly start to crave tea and cake again. This lemon one can be done in a flash without compromising on taste. It's gluten-free and with a decadent fondant texture that always calls for an extra slice.

Pre-heat your oven to 320 °F (160 °C).

In a mixing bowl, beat the coconut oil and sugar until smooth. Add the lemon zest, lemon juice, and vanilla extract, and beat again. In a separate bowl, mix the ground almonds, polenta, rice flour, baking powder, and salt. Incorporate the wet mix little by little. Finally, beat in the eggs one after the other.

Brush your cake pan with a bit of coconut oil and pour the batter into it, smoothing the top with a rubber spatula. Bake in the oven for 25 minutes, until very slightly colored. Leave to cool at room temperature before turning out on a platter.

The cake is already rather sweet, so I like to eat it with slightly tart fruits like blackberries.

Go very easy on the vanilla extract—it's here to give a rounder taste to the lemon, not to overpower it.

Always buy organic lemons when you're using the zest.

Pre-cooked polenta needs only a couple minutes' cooking time. Don't use the raw kind for this recipe as it won't be moist enough.

FOR A 10 IN. (24 CM)-DIAMETER CAKE PAN
PREPARATION TIME 15 MINUTES
COOKING TIME 25 MINUTES

2

I WELCOME THE ADVENTURE OF COOKING ABROAD
WITH GREAT EXCITEMENT, JUST AS I LOVE MAKING
THE BEST OF EVERY KITCHEN SCENARIO.
OVER-EQUIPPED OR SPARTAN, WITH FANCY
DINNERWARE OR THE BEST DISHWASHING VIEWS,
EACH MEAL COOKED IN THESE SOMETIMES-PERILOUS
CONDITIONS IS A REWARD IN ITSELF.

1   A dream of a kitchen on Okinawa island in Japan, minimalistic, open on nature and filled with handmade ceramics.

2   In a wooden cabin in Romania, a minuscule kitchen that made up for its impractical nature with an uncanny fairy-tale atmosphere.

IN THE DEEP PURPLES OF THE SEASON'S OFFERINGS,
I SEE A SUMMER THAT IS STILL LINGERING, AND
THE LAST HOURS OF CAREFREE ABUNDANCE BEFORE
THE LONG REST OF THE COLD MONTHS.

1   With the heat receding, frying eggplants in olive oil isn't a hassle anymore. Topped with a drizzle of white balsamic vinegar, they're delicious on their own.

2   In September, the vineyards facing our house are heavy with wine grapes so sweet you would confuse them with table ones.

LATE

FALL

Summer here doesn't go gently. Instead, in a meltdown of violent rains and thunderstorms, it says its goodbyes with much drama. It's the little-known face of the Mediterranean, when all the tourists are gone and its terrible temper comes out in bursts. I somehow like the intensity of it: the thirsty soil finally soaked, the moss and mushrooms coming back, and in between, like peace offerings, glorious days of sunshine to show off the golds and the reds of the leaves.

This contrasted and unpredictable weather makes fall a somehow emotional time, one that brings out sentimental recipes connected to memories, where the idea comforts as much as the taste. Mushrooms are the season's novelty, and with them come the winter squash, the sweet potatoes, the pears, the persimmons … It's a season to regroup and come back inside, and I can't imagine doing that without the help of a nice meal.

POLENTA WITH
WILD MUSHROOMS

INGREDIENTS

4 oz. (110 g) pre-cooked
  polenta
1 level tsp. coarse salt
1 tsp. butter
3 tbsp. olive oil
1 garlic clove, grated
1 level tbsp. unrefined
  sugar
8¾ oz. (250 g) mushrooms
  (shiitake, girolles or
  saffron milk caps),
  cleaned and cut in
  slices
1 tbsp. brousse or ricotta
1⅖ oz. (40 g) Parmigiano-
  Reggiano, grated
salt, pepper

I confess that knowing the heavy fall rains are helping the vegetation build stronger roots sometimes isn't enough to sit patiently through them. What seems to help, though, is to think about the immediate rewards: the wild mushrooms that will grace the market stalls a few days later. In the humid cold of these days I often crave something with a deep, comforting taste—the kind of dish that would need to cook for a long time. This polenta and mushroom combination gets me there in less than ten minutes and one could almost feel guilty about how quick and rewarding it is.

Put the equivalent of 4 times the volume of polenta in water to boil in a saucepan. Add the coarse salt.

Heat up the butter and oil in a non-stick pan, add the garlic and sugar and allow to cook on medium-high heat for a couple of minutes, until fragrant. Put the mushrooms in the pan, stir to coat them, add pepper but don't salt them yet. Leave to cook until caramelized on medium heat for 7 minutes without stirring too much. Add salt only once they're done, to keep them from getting watery.

While the mushrooms are cooking, put the polenta in the boiling water, whisking as you do. Don't stop stirring. It should be ready in 2–3 minutes. Once ready, turn off the heat, add the brousse or ricotta, half the parmigiano, and a good grind of pepper. Whisk until homogenous.

When the mushrooms are ready, divide the polenta in two bowls or shallow plates and top with the mushrooms, the remaining parmigiano, and a drizzle of olive oil.

If you can only find button mushrooms, add a bit more sugar and garlic to make their taste deeper.

No need to cut the smaller mushrooms, you just want the chunks to be of equal size so they cook uniformly.

Try as much as possible to avoid washing mushrooms, which will always make them a bit soggy, instead invest in mushroom brush.

SERVES 2 AS A MAIN
COOKING TIME 10 MINUTES

2

AS THE OFF-SEASON SETS IN, THERE'S ANOTHER KIND OF LEISURE TO BE ENJOYED IN THESE RESORT TOWNS OF ITALY. IN THE DESERTED GRAND HOTELS OR SITTING ALONE AT THE TERRACE OF A SEASIDE RESTAURANT, ONE MIGHT BE TEMPTED TO CURE THE MOST ELEGANT KIND OF MELANCHOLIA WITH A PLATE OF LINGUINE ALLE VONGOLE OR A TIRAMISU ...

1   In the midst of a fall morning, the Lago Maggiore and its mythic hotel-lined shore recovers its cinematic quality.

2   In the elegant Ligurian town of Chiavari, the most gracious kind of fall in the midst of palm trees and Liberty mansions.

ALMOND PESTO SPAGHETTI WITH
CARAMELIZED FENNEL

INGREDIENTS

FOR THE SPAGHETTI

1 fennel head
4 tbsp. olive oil
1 level tbsp. unrefined
   sugar
9 oz. (250 g) spaghetti

FOR THE PESTO

5¼ oz. (150 g) toasted
   almonds
1¾ oz. (50 g) Parmigiano-
   Reggiano, roughly
   cut in chunks
1 small garlic clove,
   grated
2 tbsp. olive oil
a handful of basil leaves
salt, pepper

This is my go-to pasta recipe for most of the year, except in the summer, when tomatoes manage to outshine my love for fennel. I only really discovered fennel a few years ago but it's been a love affair ever since. I like it raw and finely sliced but when allowed to brown and caramelize I think it turns into something irresistible. Almonds are much easier to find than pine nuts here in Provence, and for that reason they have been my favored pesto nuts for a while now. Basil, on the other hand, always tends to struggle in our dry heat, so this pesto is definitely more almonds and cheese than greens! In fact, I often complete my slim basil bounty with the wild fennel greens that seem to thrive in our garden.

Cut away the hard stems of the fennel and remove the outer layer if it's too tough. If it's tender, peeling it can be enough. Keep the green leaves for the pesto and to serve. Cut it in ½ in. (1 cm)-wide slices, removing the hard heart as you go.

Heat 4 tablespoons of olive oil in a non-stick pan with the sugar. Lay the fennel flat in the pan, avoiding too much overlap. Cover and cook on high heat for 3 minutes, until the fennel starts to brown nicely. Flip the slices, add more oil if it looks too dry, lower the heat, and put the lid back on. Cook until soft and brown, around 15 minutes.

Meanwhile, put a large pan of salted water to boil for the spaghetti.

Put the toasted almonds in the bowl of an electric mixer with the parmigiano and garlic. Grind to a medium powder. Add the oil, the basil, and most of the fennel greens. Mix again. Taste and season with salt and pepper.

Cook the spaghetti in the boiling water. While it cooks, check on your fennel and lower the heat even more if it's coloring too much. It should turn more and more brown, with crunchy caramelized bits. Put aside a ladleful of pasta cooking water before draining the spaghetti. While the spaghetti is in the colander, add the pesto, a bit of the cooking water, and half the cooked fennel to the pasta pot. Mix and put back on medium-low heat. Add the drained spaghetti and stir until the sauce starts to thicken a little. It should take a minute or two.

Serve in shallow plates and top with the remaining cooked fennel.

Good pasta has longer cooking times. Look for Italian labels and pasta made with semola di grano duro.

This recipe also works nicely with leeks.

SERVES 2 AS A MAIN
COOKING TIME 25 MINUTES

PIZZA WITH BUFALA AND 'NDUJA, WITH SAFFRON AND PANCETTA

INGREDIENTS

FOR THE DOUGH

1 level tsp. dry yeast
1 level tsp. unrefined
    sugar
⅔ cup (160 ml) warm water
6¾ oz. (190 g) Manitoba
    flour
2 oz. (60 g) semola flour
1 level tsp. fine salt

FOR THE BUFALA
AND 'NDUJA PIZZA

2¼ oz. (65 g) passata
    di pomodoro
1 tsp. unrefined sugar
1 tbsp. olive oil
salt, pepper
2 tbsp. 'nduja
2¾ oz. (80 g) mozzarella
    di bufala
a few basil leaves

FOR THE SAFFRON
AND PANCETTA PIZZA

3½ oz. (100 g) plain
    mozzarella, diced and
    strained for 15 minutes
¾ oz. (20 g) Parmigiano-
    Reggiano shavings
½ oz. (15 g) pancetta,
    finely sliced
1 tbsp. pine nuts
a pinch of crushed saffron
    threads infused
    in 1 tsp. of hot water
    for 10 minutes
pepper

I saw no point in trying to make pizza myself until I moved from central Paris to a small village in the countryside. From that moment on, what would have just been a cooking challenge became a matter of domestic necessity. I was made aware that we would not be able to survive without decent pizza, so I had to make it happen. I knew from the start that without a professional oven or—even better—a wood-fired one, I would not be able to replicate the pizze I loved. On the other hand, I learned that with great ingredients I could definitely do better than an average French pizzeria. The key to success is to make small investments: a pizza stone, a baking peel, and the right kind of Italian flour are must-haves. I use the Manitoba and semola varieties from organic brand Mulino Marino and this makes a world of difference. Once you have the tools and the flour, you're almost there. The last golden rule is to go very easy on the toppings and to remember that every water-based ingredient you put on your pizza might get in the way of the base becoming nice and crunchy.

Five hours before cooking, make the dough. Put the yeast, sugar, and half the warm water in a small bowl. Mix and leave to rest until it foams for 5–10 minutes.

In a large bowl mix the flours and salt. Form a well and pour in the yeast water and the rest of the warm water. Mix with a fork until a ball forms, then use your hand to knead the dough for 5 minutes, until smooth. Divide in two balls and leave them to rise in a warm place, each in their own bowl covered with plastic wrap so they don't dry out.

Pre-heat your oven at the highest temperature (conventional is better than fan-assisted), up to 570 °F (300 °C) if your oven allows it. This should take at least 15 minutes. Remember your oven must be as hot as possible for the dough to rise well.

For the first pizza:
In a small bowl mix the passata, sugar, olive oil, salt, and pepper. Using your hands, gently spread the first ball of dough on the floured baking peel. I like it to be very thin with a thicker outer layer. Spread the tomato sauce on it and scatter bits of the 'nduja. Slide it into the oven for 7–10 minutes, until the dough starts to color.

Take it out of the oven, put pieces of torn mozzarella di bufala on top and a few basil leaves. Finish with a splash of good olive oil.

For the second pizza:
Using your hands, gently spread the remaining ball of dough on the floured baking peel. Scatter the mozzarella, parmigiano, pancetta, and pine nuts. Drizzle with the saffron water and finally pepper generously. Bake in the oven for 7–10 minutes.

For this amount of yeast, 4–6 hours of resting is good. If you want it to rest longer, reduce the yeast amount slightly. Long leavening ensures a deeper taste and does away with the yeast taste you get with dough that has not had enough time to rise.

CARAMELIZED
ENDIVE SALAD

INGREDIENTS

FOR THE SALAD

4 tbsp. olive oil
1 level tbsp. floral honey
salt
4 endives, halved with
    core removed
1 oz. (30 g) walnut halves,
    roughly broken up
2 oz. (60 g) lamb's lettuce
3½ oz. (100 g) white
    grapes, halved
2 oz. (60 g) fresh goat's
    cheese

FOR THE DRESSING

2 tbsp. walnut oil
1 tbsp. white balsamic
    vinegar
salt, pepper

I guess getting old is waking up one day thinking my mother is right and browned endive is a great idea. I'm probably not so old that I'd go head-first into the sourness, so, yes, this recipe is more sweet and sour, but also surprisingly delicate, almost flowery. I'll confess I looked down on endive before, and the French expression "pale as an endive" probably didn't help. But that was until my father started growing endive in his cellar. Seeing their dainty tips emerging from the black soil and understanding how they were growing in the darkness, in nothing more than a crate, suddenly made them a wonder in my eyes, an example of winter resilience. Gone was the memory of the grimace-inducing endive from the school cafeteria, replaced by the sight of this homegrown delicacy.

Heat up the olive oil on high heat in a non-stick pan. Add the honey and a pinch of salt and add the endive cut-side down. Cover and leave to cook for 5 minutes, until they start to color nicely. Flip them and cook for 5 more minutes before lowering the heat and letting them soften for 15 more minutes.

Meanwhile, toast your walnuts in a pan until light brown and fragrant.

Prepare the salad dressing in a large bowl by mixing the walnut oil, vinegar, and a bit of salt and pepper. Put the lamb's lettuce, grapes, and cooled-down walnuts on top. Wait until the endive is ready to mix.

When the endive is done, divide it between two plates and arrange the salad on top. Scatter with fresh goat's cheese.

I generally remember the existence of walnut oil when the leaves start to turn yellow, right when I need the comfort of its almost sweet taste. It's too delicate to be cooked, but used raw it will help soften the bitter taste of chicory.

SERVES 2 AS A LIGHT MEAL
COOKING TIME 20 MINUTES

BUTTERNUT SQUASH AND MUSHROOMS ON JAPANESE RICE

INGREDIENTS

5½ oz. (160 g) Japanese koshihikari rice
8 tbsp. sesame or coconut oil
2 garlic cloves, thinly sliced
1 tbsp. coriander seeds
1 tsp. Aleppo pepper
1 tbsp. paprika powder
1 heaped tbsp. unrefined sugar
1 lb. 4 oz. (580 g) butternut squash, peeled and cut in ⅛ in. (½ cm) slices
1 in. (3 cm) fresh ginger, grated
4½ oz. (130 g) button mushrooms, cut in ⅛ in. (½ cm) slices
salt, pepper
2 spring onions, finely sliced
a splash of ponzu sauce

Returning from a long trip, I always feel an unbridled enthusiasm at the idea of coming back to French produce with a fresh eye. In these in-between moments, cooking feels special; you're still filled with the foreign tastes of your trip while being comforted to rediscover ones you may have been taking for granted. More than trying to accurately recreate dishes I've eaten—an often disappointing path—I try to revisit or make up new ones loosely inspired by what I've just experienced. They tend to start as simple, almost naïve, constructions, but the good ones will slowly morph into full-fledged dishes that accompany us for years.
I can't say I've specifically eaten butternut squash with rice during a recent trip we took to the Japanese countryside, but every time I make this recipe, the smell of the rice cooking, the bright orange of the squash, and the dainty spring onions take me back there again.

Rinse your rice until the water runs clear. Leave it to soak until ready to cook (10–30 minutes) while you peel the vegetables.

Heat up 4 tablespoons of oil in a non-stick pan on medium-high heat. Add the garlic, coriander seeds, Aleppo pepper, and paprika. When the garlic is turning slightly golden, add the sugar, butternut squash, and ginger. Mix with a wooden spatula to coat with the fragrant oil. Add salt and pepper. Cover and leave to cook for 10 minutes, checking regularly. The squash should start to brown.

Add the mushrooms, mix, add the remaining 4 tablespoons of oil, cover again, and cook for 15 minutes. The squash should be tender but not broken down and the mushrooms slightly caramelized.

While the squash and mushrooms finish cooking, put your rice to cook in a saucepan. If it has soaked, adding one and a half its volume of salted water should be enough. Cover and cook for 10 minutes. If it's ready before the squash, leave it in the saucepan with the lid on so it stays moist.

When ready to eat, divide the rice in two bowls and top with the cooked squash and mushrooms and sprinkle with the spring onions. Add a splash of ponzu sauce to each bowl and enjoy.

Ponzu sauce is a citrus-based (often yuzu) soy sauce found in Japanese stores. Like soy sauce it keeps for months in the fridge. If you don't have it on hand, use regular tamari sauce mixed with a bit of lemon juice.

SERVES 2 AS A MAIN
SOAKING TIME 30 MINUTES   PREPPING TIME 15 MINUTES
COOKING TIME 20 MINUTES

2

WHILE THE VALLEY RETAINS MUCH OF ITS
BLUISH-GREENS, THE MOUNTAINS NORTH OF THE
HOUSE ARE SWEPT BY A WAVE OF GOLDEN LEAVES.

1   A view of the Saoû forest and its peaks.

2   Coming in all kinds of colors and patterns, the autumn leaves always make for interesting bouquets.

SWEET POTATO
LATKES

INGREDIENTS

FOR THE LATKES

12¼ oz. (350 g) sweet
    potato, grated
1 egg
1½ tbsp. Aleppo pepper
1 tbsp. all-purpose flour
1 oz. (30 g) Emmental,
    grated
3 tbsp. olive oil
3 level tbsp. polenta
salt, pepper

FOR THE SALAD

3 tbsp. olive oil
juice of half a lime
1 small garlic clove,
    grated
3½ oz. (100 g)
    pomegranate seeds
1¼ oz. (35 g) lamb's
    lettuce
¼ oz. (10 g) fresh
    coriander, chopped

Back when I was a very young girl hassling my grandmother for yet another plate of fried potatoes, she used to remind me that another kind of potato existed. An almost mythical one for sure, since it was called sweet. In my child's mind, it was just a tale. I had grown accustomed to the elusive components of my grandmother's food stories, like the allegedly delicious greengages that never grew on her tree and the île flottante that was too challenging to attempt twice. It would be years before I finally ate sweet potato and from then proceeded to make it a common occurrence in my kitchen.
This recipe makes fall into the bright and generous season it can be. The trick is not to be shy with the seasoning to balance the sweetness of the potato. Aleppo pepper, lime juice, coriander: these will make the dish vibrant.

Pre-heat your oven to 400 °F (200 °C).

With a paper towel, soak up any extra moisture in your grated sweet potato. Transfer to a bowl and mix with the egg, Aleppo pepper, flour, salt, and Emmental. Add a generous amount of pepper.

Brush a baking tray with half the olive oil. Sprinkle half the polenta on it. Divide your potato mix into 8 galette-shaped heaps. Sprinkle the rest of the polenta and drizzle the remaining oil on top of them. Bake in the oven for 15 minutes before carefully turning them over with a spatula and cooking for 10 more minutes, until the edges are brown and crispy.

When the latkes are almost done, prepare the salad in a mixing bowl. Mix the olive oil, lime juice, and garlic, then add the pomegranate, lamb's lettuce, and fresh coriander.

Serve the latkes with the salad.

The polenta will make the latkes a little bit crispier.

If you can't find lamb's lettuce, you can also use endives.

Be generous with the fresh coriander— the salad should be really fragrant.

For a bigger meal, double the latke quantities and top with a spoonful of labneh or thick Greek yogurt.

SERVES 2 AS A LIGHT MEAL (8 SMALL LATKES)
COOKING TIME 25 MINUTES

WALNUT AND SESAME CHEESECAKE
WITH DATE SYRUP AND FIGS

INGREDIENTS

FOR THE CRUST

1¼ oz. (35 g) butter, softened

¾ oz. (20 g) whole tahini

1⅖ oz. (40 g) unrefined sugar

3 oz. (80 g) einkorn flour

a pinch of fleur de sel

1¾ oz. (50 g) walnuts, chopped

1 tbsp. sesame seeds

FOR THE FILLING

8½ oz. (240 g) brousse cheese

3½ oz. (100 g) crème fraîche

3½ oz. (100 g) Greek yogurt

1 oz. (30 g) golden sugar

2 egg whites

a few ripe black figs, to serve

date syrup, to serve

I brought date syrup home from a trip to Egypt many years ago. The whole idea was exciting but back then I struggled to incorporate it into my daily cooking. As it often happens, I looked at the precious elixir in the beautiful bottle and was unwilling to waste it on experiments. Back then I didn't know these stories always end with the hard-earned product going bad before you can find a good enough occasion to eat it. Now I know: life's too short, just use the syrup.

Cheesecake in itself is already really satisfying, but pairing it with ripe figs and the subtle taste of date syrup turns it into a much more sophisticated affair. Here, the sesame and walnut crust reminds me of the taste of Middle Eastern halva. In contrast to its sweetness, I like to keep the filling barely sweetened, ever so slightly sour from the taste of fresh cheese.

First, prepare the crust. With a fork, mix the butter in a bowl with the tahini before adding the sugar, flour, fleur de sel, walnuts, and sesame seeds. Transfer the ball of dough to your baking pan and gently press it into the bottom, forming an even layer. Put in the freezer for 1 hour.

Pre-heat your oven to 350 °F (180 °C). Inside, put an oven-proof dish filled with water. It should be big enough to hold your cheesecake tin. This will be your bain-marie. Be careful not to fill it too much or the water will overflow when you put the cheesecake in it.

Prepare the filling by putting all the ingredients in a large mixing bowl and beating vigorously (using an electric mixer is easier) until creamy and homogenous. Spread the filling on top of the cold crust.

Open the oven and delicately put the tin in the bain-marie. Let it bake for 30 minutes. The surface should not color. Once cooked, let it cool down in the turned-off oven with the door open. This will keep it from cracking.

Once at room temperature transfer to the fridge for at least 4 hours before eating. The cheesecake can also be made the day before eating.

Serve each slice with a few cut figs and a tablespoon of date syrup.

As far as the tin is concerned, I prefer to avoid hinge cake pans, which have a tendency to let the water in. Either use a pan you can cut in or line the pan with baking paper so you can take it out and flip it.

If you can't find brousse, you can replace it with ricotta or cottage cheese.

Cheesecake obviously welcomes seasonal variations. In the spring I enjoy it with a slightly tangy raspberry coulis and fresh strawberries.

Date syrup can be found in Middle Eastern stores and provides a great alternative to maple syrup on pancakes.

You can fold the leftover egg yolks into a pie crust or use them to make sablés.

SERVES 4–6 PEOPLE

MAKES A 7 IN. (17 CM)-DIAMETER, 2 IN. (5 CM)-HIGH CHEESECAKE

FREEZING TIME 1 HOUR   PREPPING TIME 20 MINUTES   COOKING TIME 30 MINUTES

1

I LIKE THE FRAGILE BEAUTY OF A
WILD FALL BOUQUET WITH ITS LEAVES AND
PISTILS HOLDING ON BY A THREAD.

1 Spindle berries, wild clematis, and a lichen-covered branch bring the chance encounters of an unkempt garden inside.

2 Cold mornings call for warm sweaters that are shed away by midday when the sun has warmed the house.

2

AFTER A DAY OF HEAVY RAIN, THE SUN HAS A WAY
TO MIRACULOUSLY APPEAR AT SUNSET IN A
BURST OF ORANGE LIGHT IN A TESTAMENT TO THE
MEDITERRANEAN FALL'S UNPREDICTABLE MOODS.

1 This time of year, the light shows coincide with the preparation of dinner.

2 Warm rays playing with the brass and woody tones of the house.

EARLY

WINTER

When the rains stop, temperatures drop, and the skies clear up, I know winter is close. I welcome it with a sigh of relief because it's a return to calmness after a few weeks of intense downpours. The clouds are swept away by the winds and as I emerge from my fall *ermitage*, the horizon feels immense. It's time to venture outside again and explore wild tracks and crest trails. Solstice days here can be short and blindingly bright, offering a stunning shot of sunlight to sustain you through the long nights.

I go to great lengths to convince myself that winter meals can be vibrant and fragrant in addition to heartwarming. More than in any other season, I want them to provide an escape, to hint at cuisines from further south. There is even some excitement in revisiting the winter produce I had almost forgotten during the warmer months: carrots, leeks, endive, onions, fennel, chickpeas…

It's always a richer palette than I give it credit for.

FENNEL, CHICKPEA, AND LEMON TAGINE

INGREDIENTS

FOR THE TAGINE

8 tbsp. olive oil
1 level tbsp. harissa paste
1 tbsp. ground cumin
1 tbsp. ground coriander
1 tsp. ground turmeric
2 large garlic cloves,
    finely chopped
1 small preserved lemon,
    rinsed
1 small fennel head,
    peeled and chopped
    in 2 in. (5 cm) strips
3½ oz. (100 g) canned
    chickpeas, rinsed
    and drained
7 oz. (200 g) canned
    tomatoes
1⅓ oz. (40 g) golden raisins
1 cup (230 ml) water
salt, pepper
a few coriander sprigs,
    to serve

FOR THE COUSCOUS

3½ oz. (100 g) medium
    semolina
¼ oz. (10 g) butter
salt

When I think of winter in Morocco, I think of blinding sun, peaceful evergreen gardens, and the silhouette of the snow-capped Atlas Mountains in the distance. There is something a bit unreal about it, as if the weather has come to a halt on the edge of winter, right before the real coldness begins. It is a rather blissful state, one that always comes to my mind when the light is especially bright on these first days of Provençal winter, and it calls for a heartwarming and sunny vegetarian tagine. Slow-cooked, fragrant, and spicy vegetables paired with delicate semolina never fail to uplift me.

Heat the olive oil on medium heat in a non-stick skillet. Add the harissa, cumin, coriander, ground turmeric, garlic, and lemon. Mix with a wooden spatula and leave to cook for a couple of minutes until fragrant.

Add the fennel, chickpeas, and a pinch of pepper, stir to coat well, and leave to cook covered for 5 minutes.

Remove the lid and add the tomatoes, raisins, and water. Mix, cover again, and leave to cook on medium heat for 60 minutes, checking regularly. The fennel should be soft and slightly translucent. If it starts to stick, add a bit more water or lower the heat. Toward the end, taste to see if it needs salt or if the preserved lemon was salty enough.

When the tagine is almost done, cook the semolina. Put the dry semolina in a bowl along with a pinch of salt. Add the volume of semolina in boiling water and cover with a plate. A few minutes later, remove the plate and gently fluff it up with a fork. Add the butter and mix carefully.

To serve, put the semolina next to the tagine and top with a few coriander sprigs.

For this recipe I like to use canned datterini tomatoes from Italian brands like Così Com'è.

Semolina tastes very different from one brand to the next. Look for Moroccan brands such as Dari in Middle Eastern stores.

If you own an earthenware casserole you can use it for this recipe, just be sure not to turn the heat too high.

This kind of recipe can be done in advance and always benefits from cooking a little longer or being reheated.

This can be turned into a heartwarming soup by adding more water and tomatoes and replacing the semolina with noodles thrown in the soup at the very end.

SERVES 2 AS A MAIN
COOKING TIME 60 MINUTES

NOT-SO-SIMPLE
CARROT SOUP

INGREDIENTS

2 tbsp. olive oil
1 small garlic clove,
   roughly chopped
1 dried peperoncino,
   crushed
13¼ oz. (375 g) carrots,
   peeled and cut in ⅕ in.
   (½ cm) slices
1 level tbsp. dried oregano
scant cup (210 ml) water
1 big tbsp. Greek yogurt
juice of half a lemon
salt, pepper
1¾ oz. (50 g) hard ewe's
   cheese such as
   Manchego, in fine
   shavings, to serve
two pinches of dried
   sumac, to serve

For the longest time I made a point of not liking soup, which is probably strange for a grown woman. I'm guessing childhood experiences were to blame; taste memories are often hard to shake. I was mostly suspicious of the idea of lots of ingredients disappearing into a mysterious concoction—which, I admit, sounds like the definition of soup. This recipe is one of reconciliation for me. I like to think of it as a soup for beginners. It's very easy to put together yet sophisticated enough that you'll be proud of it.

Heat the olive oil in a non-stick saucepan, add the garlic and peperoncino, and let it color slightly. Add the carrots and oregano and season with salt and pepper. Cover and allow to simmer on medium heat for 4 minutes—it should start to smell nice. Add the water, replace the lid, and let it cook on medium-high heat for 20–30 minutes, until the carrots are tender.

Once the carrots are done, transfer to a tall container to mix with an immersion blender. Mix until smooth. Add the yogurt and lemon juice. Taste for seasoning. Adjust texture with hot water if you want it more liquid—I personally like it somewhere between a soup and a purée.

Transfer to individual bowls, top with the cheese, a pinch of sumac, and drizzle with some good olive oil.

You'll find dried sumac in Middle Eastern stores. It has a nice acidic kick and keeps for a while so it's a good thing to have in your pantry.

SERVES 2 AS A LIGHT MEAL
COOKING TIME 30 MINUTES

THE EVER-BOUNTIFUL MARKETS OF THE
SOUTHERN SIDE OF THE MEDITERRANEAN
ARE A SIGHT FOR SORE EUROPEAN EYES.
WHAT'S WINTER WHEN THE SKIES ARE
CLEAR AND THE WEATHER WARM ENOUGH
FOR THE STALLS TO BE SO PLENTIFUL?

1   In the old Souk of Aswan in Egypt one can only marvel at the variety of products grown along the Nile's fertile shores.

2   A truckful of pomegranates in the perpetual open-air market of the streets of Marrakech.

LEEK AND HARISSA SHAKSHUKA
ON FLATBREAD

INGREDIENTS

FOR THE FLATBREAD

4½ oz. (125 g) whole
    wheat flour
1½ tbsp. fennel seeds
1½ tbsp. coriander seeds
½ tsp. fine salt
½ tsp. baking powder
2 tbsp. olive oil
¼ cup (60 ml) water

FOR THE SHAKSHUKA

3 tbsp. olive oil
1 level tbsp. harissa paste
1 garlic clove, grated
10½ oz. (300 g) peeled and
    cleaned leeks, cut in
    ⅕ in. (½ cm) slices
generous 1 cup (280 ml)
    canned chopped
    tomatoes
1 tbsp. unrefined sugar
2 eggs
salt, pepper
¾ oz. (20 g) shaved
    Parmigiano-Reggiano,
    to serve

As the temperature drops, I start to crave the combination of fried eggs and browned vegetables. It's the perfect answer to my need for something hearty and quick to put together. This recipe gives some credit to leeks, the winter underdog of my fridge; they keep too well for their own good and always end up being the last-resort vegetable when all the others have gone. This variation on a shakshuka might even convince the leek skeptics. It sits on a fragrant flatbread whose texture resembles more of a biscuit or crust, which I think works very well with eggs.

Start by making the flatbread dough. In a bowl, mix the flour, seeds, salt, and baking powder. Make a well in the center and add the olive oil and water. Mix with a fork to form a ball. Knead it a little, just so it gets smoother. Leave the dough in a bowl to rest while you cook the eggs and sauce.

Start cooking the shakshuka sauce. Heat the olive oil in a non-stick pan over medium-high heat and add the harissa and garlic. Stir with a wooden spatula until fragrant and add the leeks along with salt and pepper. Mix to coat and leave to cook for 3 minutes, until it starts to gain some color. Lower the heat, add the tomatoes, sugar, and a couple of pinches of salt. Mix well, cover, and leave to cook for 20 minutes, until the sauce has darkened.

When your shakshuka sauce is almost ready you can start cooking the flatbread. Heat up a flat non-stick pan on very high heat. Divide the dough into two balls and use a rolling pin to spread them into 8 in. (20 cm) circles. Cook each for 3 minutes on each side, until they color a little. Once done, put each of them on a flat plate.

Make two indentations in your sauce and break the eggs into them. Cover and leave to cook for a few minutes, depending on how well done you like them. Scatter the parmigiano on top and divide between the two plates, laying the shakshuka on top of the flatbread.

If you don't have whole wheat, another flavorful flour such as einkorn or buckwheat will do. To make it easier to roll out, mix it with half of regular wheat flour.

You can skip the cheese and substitute it with fresh coriander.

This recipe welcomes many variations. A good cupboard one is to replace the leeks with chickpeas and canned peppers.

SERVES 2 AS A MAIN
COOKING TIME 30 MINUTES

CRUNCHY
WINTER SALAD

INGREDIENTS

3 tbsp. pepitas
1 tsp. fennel seeds
5 tbsp. olive oil
1 pink grapefruit, in
    peeled segments
1 small carrot, peeled
    and sliced with
    a mandoline
2 endive, core removed,
    chopped widthwise
1 small fennel,
    sliced thinly with
    a mandoline
1 tbsp. soft golden raisins
1¾oz. (50 g) Beaufort
    cheese, cut
    in small sticks
fleur de sel
pepper

Just because it's colder outside doesn't mean I'm giving up on salads. I find I really need raw meals with a crunch to balance out the soft, warm dishes that come with the season. It's also quite a relief to have a healthy weeknight dish that doesn't require any cooking and can be ready quickly.

This type of salad lends itself to many variations. Depending on my mood and what's in my fridge it might also feature apples, radishes, or dates and welcomes the addition of other nuts and seeds. I like the idea of not needing a complicated dressing, just excellent oil. I'm partial to olive but might switch things up with sesame or walnut to avoid winter-salad fatigue.

Toast the pepitas and fennel seeds in a pan until they start to pop. It should take a few minutes. Put aside.

Put the olive oil in a salad bowl. Add the grapefruit, carrot, endive, fennel, raisins, cheese, pepitas, and fennel seeds. Mix to coat with oil. Season with fleur de sel and add plenty of black pepper. Mix again and serve.

Use a good-quality, fragrant olive oil for best results.

If you can't find Beaufort, hard ewe's cheese or parmigiano works nicely too.

If you want to make it vegan, leave out the cheese and add a teaspoon of whole tahini to the dressing.

SERVES 2 AS A LIGHT MEAL
COOKING TIME 4 MINUTES

EVERY TIME A WOODEN OBJECT ENTERS MY KITCHEN IT FEELS LIKE A VICTORY OVER PLASTIC, A SOFT RESPITE FROM THE CLANG OF METAL, AND THE BEGINNING OF A LONG RELATIONSHIP. YEARS AFTER ACQUIRING THEM, I STILL RUN MY FINGERS OVER THEIR SURFACES WITH PLEASURE, LIKE I DID WITH MY MOTHER'S WORN-OUT WOODEN SPOONS.

1   A monoxyl bud vase, spreader knife, and fork from Japan sitting on a Korean stand.

2   My ever-growing collection of wooden utensils is made of heirlooms, travel finds, and artisan pieces.

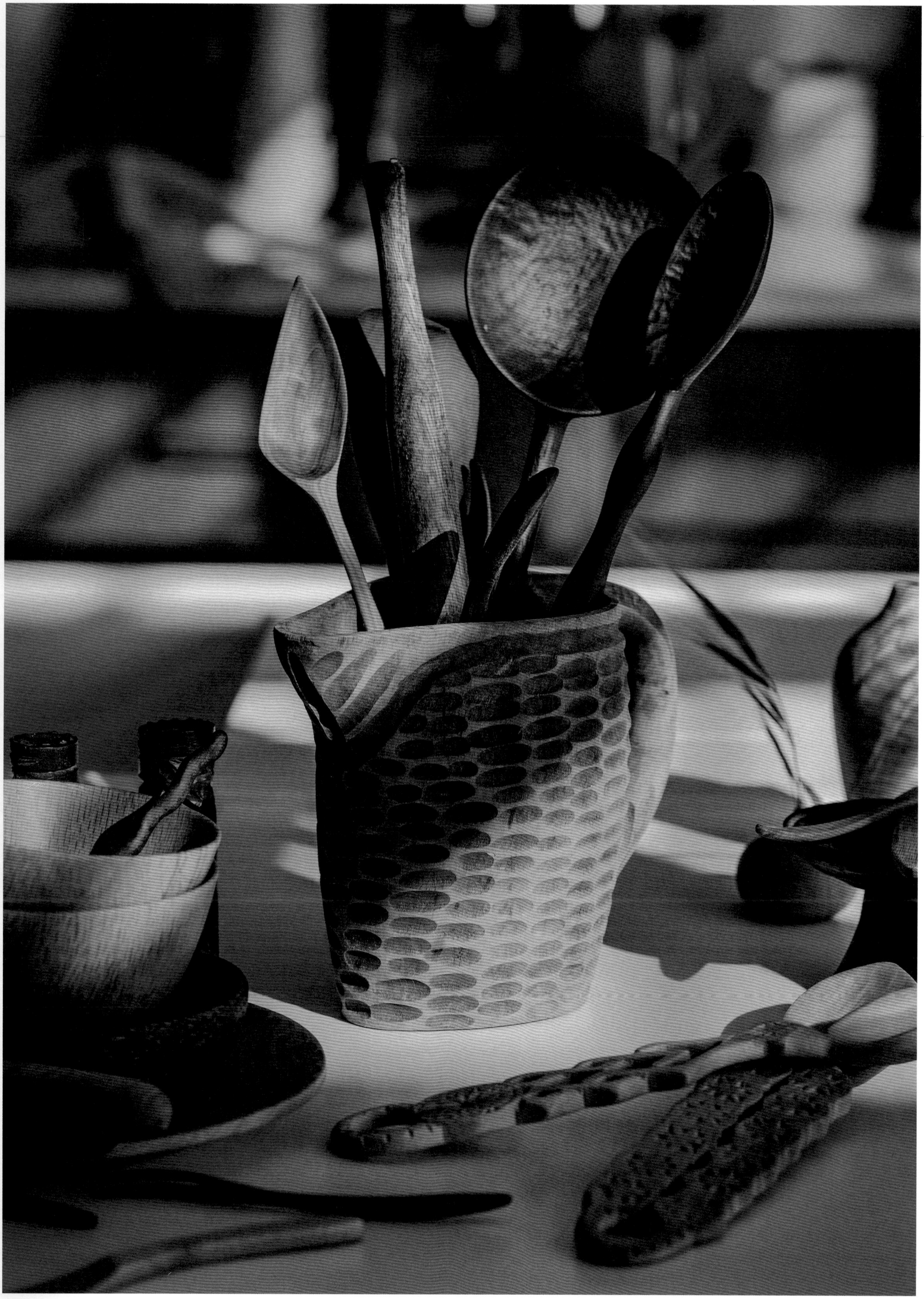

PASTA
ALLA SALSICCIA

INGREDIENTS

4 tbsp. olive oil
1 garlic clove, grated
1 tbsp. fennel seeds
7½ oz. (210 g) fresh pork
  sausage, skin removed,
  cut in chunks
2 cups (500 ml) passata
  di pomodoro
1 tbsp. unrefined sugar
a piece of Parmigiano-
  Reggiano rind
  (¾ oz./25 g)
7 oz. (200 g) dried pasta
salt, pepper
1 oz. (30 g) Parmigiano-
  Reggiano, freshly
  grated, to serve
a few basil leaves,
  to serve

One summer, we rented out an old apartment next door to the Grand Hotel Tremezzo on the Lake Como. Disheartened by the rather touristy restaurants, I set out to cook and shop from local markets and stores. Under the hot August sun, relying solely on our legs and Italian buses, the enterprise was somewhat challenging. It sometimes felt more like scavenging than shopping! Nearby was an old-school macelleria that I only dared enter with my broken Italian because options were scarce. Inside, nothing was on display but fresh fennel sausage, which I bought without being able to form a decent sentence. I brought the bounty to my kitchen de fortune and proceeded to turn it into pasta alla salsiccia, an instant success that was the proto-type of the recipe below. Fennel sausage is hard to find in France, which led me to add fennel seeds to the final recipe. I tend to cook this all year round, but its comforting nature makes it a great cold-weather dish.

In a non-stick pan, heat the olive oil on medium-high heat. Add the garlic and fennel seeds and cook until golden. Add the sausage, mix well, and cook for a few minutes, until it starts to color.

Lower the heat and add the passata, sugar, and parmigiano rind. Season with salt and pepper. Cover and cook on medium heat for 20 minutes until the sauce has thickened and turned a deeper red.

While the sauce cooks you can prepare the pasta. Bring a large pot of water to boil, add a good pinch of coarse salt. Large pasta like paccheri often takes 12–14 minutes to cook. Toward the end, take out a glass-worth of cooking water.

Take the parmigiano rind out of the sauce (in my kitchen there's usually someone more than willing to eat it on the spot).

Drain your pasta. Add a bit of cooking water to your sauce (especially if it has reduced a lot). Transfer the sauce to your emptied pasta pot and add the drained pasta. Mix thoroughly on medium heat for a few minutes, until the sauce has coated the pasta.

Divide between two shallow plates, drizzle with good olive oil, and top with a few basil leaves and grated parmigiano.

When they're in season, this can be made with fresh tomatoes—just increase the tomato quantity a little since they'll reduce more than the passata.

A tomato sauce can only benefit from cooking slowly and for a long time. If you're not in a rush, reduce the heat and cook it a little longer.

While this is also good with long pasta, I like this sauce with bigger shapes like paccheri or rigatoni.

If you don't have basil, you can add a few crushed sprigs of rosemary to the oil at the beginning.

SERVES 2 AS A MAIN
COOKING TIME 25 MINUTES

MILLET AND GOAT'S CHEESE GALETTES
WITH CRISPY RED ONION

INGREDIENTS

FOR THE GALETTES

4½ oz. (125 g) millet,
  rinsed and drained
1 small garlic clove,
  grated
¾ oz. (25 g) fresh goat's
  cheese
¾ oz. (25 g) Emmental,
  grated
1 egg
2 tbsp. olive oil
salt, pepper

FOR THE SIDES

1 red onion, thinly sliced
2 tbsp. olive oil
a pinch of Aleppo pepper
fleur de sel
1 avocado
1 tbsp. lemon juice
2 tbsp. thick Greek yogurt
2 pinches of sumac

Millet is one of those health-store cereals that might end up dying at the back of your cupboard unless you find a really good use for it. Cooked plainly, you'd be hard pressed to say it looks or tastes enticing. But don't dismiss it just yet, because once you turn it into a flavorful galette, its half-fondant, half-crispy texture really shines. Oven-roasted red onion has a way of making everything nicer, but beyond that, what I like with this recipe is that it brings color and freshness at a time of year when I really start to miss them.

Put the drained millet along with two times its volume in water in a saucepan. Add a pinch of coarse salt, cover, and cook on medium-high heat for 12 minutes, or until the water has evaporated. Turn the heat off.

Pre-heat your oven to 400 °F (200 °C). Add the garlic, goat's cheese, Emmental, and cracked egg to the cooked millet. Whisk with a fork and pepper generously.

Lay your sliced onion on a non-stick baking sheet (or on parchment paper if it isn't non-stick). Drizzle with the olive oil, Aleppo pepper, and a pinch of fleur de sel. Mix to coat. Cook in the oven for 12–14 minutes, until brown and crispy. Watch it closely as the transition between well-done and burnt can be swift. Take out of the oven once done.

Meanwhile, you can cook the galettes. Heat the olive oil in a flat non-stick pan. Using a spoon, form 4 galettes with the millet mix. Leave to cook for 5 minutes on high heat before flipping them with a wide spatula. You want them to get brown and crispy. They are a little delicate to handle the first time but if they're grilled enough they get easier to flip. In any case, they don't have to be perfect—the loose grains scattered in the pan will turn into crispy morsels and all will be good!

While the galettes are cooking, slice the avocado and drizzle with the lemon juice.

Finally, assemble all the elements. Start with the galettes, add the avocado, spoon a tablespoon of Greek yogurt on top of each plate and add a pinch of sumac. Finally, add the onions, a pinch of fleur de sel, and a drizzle of olive oil.

Whenever I'm out of millet I cook these with quinoa or semolina.

Fresh goat's cheese has a light taste—if you can only find the matured variety, reduce the amount by half.

The galettes can sit around and be reheated, so don't worry if you can't do everything simultaneously. The only thing that's best right out of the oven are the onions.

SERVES 2 AS A MAIN
COOKING TIME 25 MINUTES

FLAN WITH
EINKORN CRUST

INGREDIENTS

FOR THE CRUST

1⅖oz. (40g) all-purpose
    flour plus extra to dust
2¾oz. (80g) einkorn flour
2 level tbsp. unrefined
    sugar
a pinch of fleur de sel
2oz. (60g) butter,
    softened
2 tbsp. water

FOR THE CUSTARD

2¼oz. (65g) golden sugar
1⅕oz. (35g) corn starch
⅓ cup (80ml) whipping
    cream
1 small tsp. vanilla
    extract
1⅓ cup (330ml) full-fat
    milk
3–4 egg yolks

Flan was ubiquitous in the bakeries of my childhood. The huge slices sold then barely had any crust and were the kind of dense thing you'd eat when you were actually hungry, not just looking for something sweet. I forgot all about it as I moved out to fancier, bigger cities, where pastries were a much more dainty affair. Things came full circle with the come-back of old-school recipes on Parisian bakery counters, and I woke up one day thinking I might just crave flan again.
Making it yourself is a bit more technical than a regular cake, but I find it quite straightforward once you get the hang of the few things that guarantee success. Patience is the key! This version is more sophisticated than the rather bland slices of my childhood. It has a thicker and crunchier sablé crust made from flavorful einkorn flour and is filled with a generous custard that hovers between firm and creamy.

Start by making the crust. Mix all the dry ingredients in a bowl, form a well, add the butter and water and gently mix it with a fork until you can form a ball. Don't overwork the dough. Cover with plastic wrap and put in the fridge. It will be easier to spread once colder.

Now prepare the custard. With the heat turned off, mix the sugar and corn starch in a saucepan. Add the whipping cream and whisk until smooth. Add the vanilla and milk and whisk again. Finally, add the egg yolks, making sure you have the right weight.

Cook the custard mixture over medium heat. It should not boil but still be warm enough for the cream to cook. Whisk it gently for 15 minutes, waiting for it to thicken. Once it has reached the consistency of crème fraîche, turn the heat off and transfer to a shallow bowl to cool down.

Take the dough out of the fridge and roll it out on a lightly floured surface before putting it in the cake an with the help of your rolling pin. This recipe calls for a rather thick crust which will also make the fragile dough easier to handle. Cover the cake pan with plastic wrap and put in the freezer for 2 hours.

Cover the custard with plastic wrap, making sure it touches the surface of the custard to avoid any condensation. Refrigerate for 2 hours.

Pre-heat your oven to 350°F (175°C). Take out the crust from the freezer and the custard from the fridge. Remove plastic wrap, gently whisk the cream to make it more homogenous and transfer it into the crust using a rubber spatula. Smooth out the surface and bake in the oven for 45 minutes, until the top starts to turn light brown. Let it cool at room temperature for at least 3 hours before eating. Keep in the fridge after the first day.

For the flan's texture to be a success, ingredients are key. Farm eggs, full-fat milk, and quality cream are essential. Steer clear of any light dairy for this to work.

I use an artisanal variety of vanilla extract. If you can't find good-quality extract, you can also grate a vanilla bean into the custard before cooking.

Using a cake pan with a removable bottom will make your life easier.

2

THE WINTER SUN IS STRETCHING SHADOWS, MAKING MIDDAY LOOK LIKE A NEVER-ENDING AFTERNOON.

1   Outside, the water has stopped running down the rain chains.

2   On the table, a glorious branch of cotinus catches the light.

2

WARM BROWNS COME TO
LIFE IN THE WINTER SUN.

1   Horses in the fleeting evening light.

2   The branches of broom shrubs are often dry after the summer droughts, creating graphic silhouettes.

LATE

WINTER

Growing up in the north of France, it felt like winter's austere palette was only the dark brown of leafless trees and the dirty white of the sky. Here in Provence, with the evergreen foliage of the white oaks, pines, and junipers, green never disappears. Still, the colors do shift, and with no small amount of subtlety. The frosted blue of lavenders, the gold of giant canes, the pale greens of olive trees, the orange bark of a young tree, all arrange themselves in a complex seasonal array of pastels that seem to get paler as the cold gets stronger.

The sun does make glorious appearances, and lures you into thinking that surely nature is ready to revive itself at any second. It's only a sunny mirage though; the season has to run its course.

In the kitchen I grow a bit restless, and the only novelty comes from the long-awaited citrus season. Anything is good to help with the wait for spring: let's open these pantry treasures I've been keeping for hard times—jars of jams, tomatoes, and artichokes—let's have cake and biscuits every day. Hard times are almost over, and we might still have a few good winter meals in us before the strawberries finally come.

ORANGE AND
RED ONION SALAD

INGREDIENTS

¼ oz. (10 g) whole almonds,
    cut lengthwise
5 tbsp. olive oil
1 tsp. dried oregano
half a small red onion,
    very thinly sliced
3 small table oranges,
    in peeled segments
salt, pepper
a few radicchio leaves,
    to serve

The first time I ate an orange salad was in a small restaurant in Modica, Sicily. It was one of those merciless, cold, and windy days when it feels like the Mediterranean is done playing nice and throws winter at you without warning. Insalata di arance rang like a luxury to my northern ears. I didn't expect the unceremonious peasant fare that ended up in front of me: oranges cut roughly in a rustic, shallow plate, as though this was just any other winter salad. Ah, but that was the genius of it! It's disarmingly simple—oranges with olive oil and plenty of salt and pepper—but for me it opened up something. In the dead of winter it's sometimes hard to feel like any of the fresh produce is an indulgence. But this salad, with a side of good bread and cheese, can lift you up a little. To stay true to the bold idea of an orange-only salad, I like the radicchio to be a supporting character in this dish, adding only a few leaves to balance the sweetness of the orange.

Toast the almonds in a pan until slightly golden. Put aside.

In a salad bowl, mix the olive oil and oregano. Add the sliced onions and oranges. Salt and pepper generously. Add the radicchio leaves, mix gently to coat with the olive oil and serve immediately.

Cutting the orange in peeled segments requires a sharp knife and a bit of patience. When I'm not feeling that fancy, I simply remove the outer skin and the pith and cut it in slices. It's somehow truer to the dish's not-so-precious origins.

Depending on what I find in the market, I also use grapefruit, blood oranges, or a mix of citrus.

SERVES 2 AS A LIGHT MEAL
COOKING TIME 5 MINUTES

IT'S A STRIKING THING SEEING CITRUS ON A
TREE FOR THE FIRST TIME. YOU'D THINK IT WOULD
DISPEL THE MAGIC, THAT CITRUS WOULD STOP
BEING THIS MYSTERIOUS WINTER OFFERING FROM
DISTANT WARMER LANDS. BUT IN MY
EYES IT BECOMES ALL THE MORE MIRACULOUS.

1   Lemons on a market stall in Egypt.
2   A yuzu orchard on the sub-tropical island of Yakushima, Japan.

PAPPA
AL POMODORO

INGREDIENTS

7 tbsp. olive oil

1 sweet onion, finely diced

1 garlic clove, diced

1 peperoncino

1 small carrot, finely diced

1 tbsp. unrefined sugar

1 oz. (30 g) sun-dried tomatoes in oil, chopped

1 lb. (450 g) polpa di pomodoro or canned tomatoes

a piece of Parmigiano-Reggiano rind (¾ oz./20 g)

3½ oz. (100 g) closed-crumb bread such as einkorn, diced in ½ in. (1 cm) pieces (stale is good!)

salt, pepper

2 tbsp. pitted taggiasche olives

1¼ oz. (35 g) Parmigiano-Reggiano shavings

a few basil leaves (optional)

Tomatoes might be the thing I miss most in winter. To compensate, I keep a pantry filled with preserved tomatoes of all kinds: homemade jars of sauce, bottles of passata and polpa, cans of peeled datterini, and bags and jars of dried tomatoes. It's somewhere between a museum and a gourmet survivalist's cave, and it's what I need to wait out the winter.

This simple recipe comes from a classic of Italian peasant cooking—a soup made from bread and tomatoes. As so often with these popular recipes, it starts to feel very luxurious if you're careful to pick good ingredients. Topped with good olives and parmigiano, it turns a weeknight meal into something special.

Heat 3 tablespoons of olive oil in a saucepan on medium-high heat. Put in the onion, garlic, peperoncino, carrot, sugar, and sun-dried tomatoes. Stir with a wooden spoon and cook for 10 minutes until the onions are soft and golden.

Add the tomatoes, parmigiano rind, salt, and pepper. Go light on the salt. Stir and leave to cook on medium heat for 30 minutes, covering halfway through, so it doesn't reduce too much.

When the soup is almost done, prepare the croutons. Heat the remaining 4 tablespoons of olive oil on high heat in a pan, drop the diced bread in, and season with salt and pepper. Cook for 5 minutes until golden.

Add a little less than half of the croutons to the saucepan and put the rest aside. Blend the soup with a hand mixer. Beware of splashes, it will be hot!

Divide the soup between two bowls and top with the olives, parmigiano shavings, remaining croutons, and basil leaves. Add a splash of good olive oil if you're feeling decadent. Enjoy while it's hot.

This can also be made using fresh tomatoes with varieties such as San Marzano or Roma. I just rarely happen to crave soup when fresh tomatoes are still on the market stalls!

You can also replace the parmigiano shavings with a spoonful of stracciatella or ricotta.

If your basil pot is long gone, try putting a few rosemary sprigs in the oil at the beginning of the recipe instead.

SERVES 2 AS A LIGHT MEAL
COOKING TIME 40 MINUTES

BRIGHT WINTER SALAD
WITH KUMQUAT

INGREDIENTS

1 oz. (30 g) cashews
1 tbsp. pepitas
1 tsp. sesame oil
1 tbsp. rice vinegar
3 tbsp. olive oil
4 tbsp. ponzu sauce
2 oz. (60 g) kumquats,
    halved, deseeded,
    finely sliced
1⅓ oz. (40 g) mixed baby
    leaves (rucola, lamb's
    lettuce, radicchio ...)
1 avocado, cut in
    ⅕ in. (½ cm) slices
fleur de sel
pepper

The kumquat, despite its fancy tropical appearance, is actually quite cold-hardy. This explains how it can make a surprise appearance on the stands of my local farmers' market at a time when fruits are few and far between. This prompts an urge to put them in everything, in an attempt to get out of winter's cooking slump. In this simple recipe, and with a bit of help from ponzu sauce, they manage to make the idea of avocado salad tempting again.

In a small pan, toast the cashews and pepitas with the sesame oil until golden. It should only take a few minutes.

In a salad bowl, mix the rice vinegar, olive oil, and ponzu sauce. Add the kumquats, baby leaves, avocado, cashews, pepitas, a pinch of fleur de sel and pepper. Gently mix to coat with the dressing. Serve immediately.

For this salad it's nice to have a rich mix of leaves, some sweet and some more bitter. You can also add finely chopped endive.

If you can't find ponzu sauce, try mixing tamari sauce with kumquat juice.

This salad pairs well with smoked salmon on toast.

SERVES 2 AS A LIGHT MEAL
COOKING TIME 5 MINUTES

PIADINA WITH BROCCOLI AND COPPA

INGREDIENTS

FOR THE PIADINA

1¾ oz. (50 g) 00 flour, plus
    extra to dust
1¾ oz. (50 g) semola flour
¼ tsp. baking powder
½ tsp. fine salt
3½ tbsp. warm water
1½ tbsp. olive oil

FOR THE FILLING

7 oz. (200 g) mozzarella
    di bufala, cut in slices
1¼ oz. (35 g) coppa
5 tbsp. olive oil
1 garlic clove, grated
a pinch of a smoky chili
    such as chipotle morita
7 oz. (200 g) broccoli,
    broken into small
    florets
salt, pepper

Piadina is an Italian flatbread from the Emilia-Romagna region. I had it first on my honeymoon a few years ago, on a night we were looking for pizza and found this instead. In Italy, straying off the path has a way of leading to cherished discoveries. Piadina is as good as the flour you use and the ingredients you put inside. It's quickly put together and it might just ease that pizza craving when it's way too late to wait for dough to rise.

First, make the piadina dough. In a bowl, mix all the dry ingredients with a fork. Form a well and add the water and olive oil. Mix to form a ball and knead with your hands for 5 minutes until the dough is smooth. Cover the bowl with a towel and leave to rest for 30 minutes.

When the dough has rested, prepare the coppa and mozzarella so they're ready and at room temperature for later.

Cook the broccoli. Heat the olive oil on medium-high heat in a non-stick pan, add the garlic, chili, and broccoli florets. Stir to coat them in the oil. Add salt and pepper and cook covered for 8 minutes, stirring them a few times. The florets should be cooked through but not soft, with brown and crispy edges.

While the broccoli is cooking, heat up a flat pan to cook the piadine. Divide the dough in two and spread out on a lightly floured surface into 8 in. (20 cm) circles. Cook them on high heat one after the other, a couple of minutes on each side. They should only color slightly. Transfer each to a flat plate, fill them with the mozzarella, the coppa, and the broccoli. Drizzle with olive oil and fold them in two before serving.

00 flour is the Italian equivalent of pastry flour. The semola flour makes the dough more flavorful but if you can't find it, use only 00.

If you can get your hands on some broccolini, these would work beautifully here.

This is just one variation on the piadina, the whole concept is easy to adapt all year long.

This can become a vegetarian meal by replacing the coppa with rucola or sun-dried tomatoes.

SERVES 2 AS A MAIN
RESTING TIME 30 MINUTES
COOKING TIME 8–10 MINUTES

POLENTA AND SAFFRON FRIES
WITH BRUSSELS SPROUTS

INGREDIENTS

FOR THE FRIES

two pinches of saffron
    threads
1½ oz. (45 g) pre-cooked
    polenta
1½ oz. (45 g) grated
    Parmigiano-Reggiano
salt, pepper
olive oil, to brush

FOR THE SPROUTS

5 tbsp. olive oil
a handful of sage leaves
1 tbsp. unrefined sugar
12¼ oz. (350 g) brussels
    sprouts, peeled and
    halved
2 tbsp. fresh brousse
    (optional), to serve

The end of winter is the toughest time of the year, fresh-produce-wise. Any novelty, or illusion of it, feels like a godsend. I'm guessing this explains why I tend to welcome the arrival of the brussels sprout with a little too much enthusiasm. Maybe it's just that I still can't wrap my head around the fact that this former childhood monster can taste so good? Fried in oil and slightly caramelized, they become my veggie of choice, with rice and soy sauce, with eggs, or, as here, with polenta.
Turning polenta into fries requires a bit of patience but barely any work. I like the idea of making them into something comforting yet luxurious by adding saffron threads, a surefire way to light up a winter plate.

Grind the saffron to a powder in a mortar and add 2 tablespoons of hot water. Put aside.

Cook the polenta—this needs to be made ahead of time so it can set. Put four times the volume of polenta into water to boil in a saucepan. Salt well with coarse salt. Pour the polenta slowly in the water, whisking as you go. Pre-cooked polenta takes 2–3 minutes to cook on high heat. Switch off the heat as soon as it gets creamy. Add the parmigiano, saffron water, and season generously with pepper. Whisk to incorporate.

Oil a rectangular dish (11 × 8 in./28 × 21 cm) and spread the polenta in it, smoothing the surface with a rubber spatula. Let it cool at room temperature then cover and chill in the fridge for at least 1 hour and 30 minutes (it can be overnight).

Once the polenta has set, pre-heat your oven to 420 °F (220 °C).

Flip the slab of polenta out onto a cutting board and cut it into 1 in. (2½ cm)-wide fries. Arrange them on a baking tray and brush them with a little olive oil. Bake in the oven for 20 minutes until golden on the edges.

Meanwhile, cook the brussels sprouts. Heat the olive oil in a non-stick pan on high heat. Sizzle the sage leaves for a couple of minutes before adding the sugar and sprouts. Mix with a spatula to coat them in oil, and season with salt and pepper. Cover and cook them on high heat for 5 minutes until they have some color. Lower the heat and cook for 10 more minutes, until tender and browned.

Once ready, divide the fries and sprouts between two plates and if you feel so inclined, top with a tablespoon of fresh brousse.

These polenta fries work well with melt-in-the mouth browned vegetables like fennel or, when they are in season, zucchini.

SERVES 2 AS A MAIN
COOKING TIME 20 MINUTES
RESTING TIME 1 HOUR AND 30 MINUTES

HONEY AND
ANISEED SABLÉS

INGREDIENTS

2¾ oz. (80 g) einkorn flour
1½ oz. (40 g) semola flour
1 oz. (30 g) ground
   almonds
a pinch of fleur de sel
1 tsp. aniseed powder
1 tbsp. fennel seeds,
   plus a few to sprinkle
2¾ oz. (80 g) butter,
   softened
2 tbsp. mild honey such
   as lavender
a few whole almonds,
   chopped

One life goal of mine is to always have a jar filled with fresh biscuits on my kitchen counter. It sounds like a bit of a commitment, but, still, isn't it one of the most attainable ways to create a fairy-tale kitchen?
I like my sablés to melt in the mouth and am wary of good-looking but ultimately dry biscuits. To get to that soft texture, good butter and ground almonds are a sure bet. With the addition of lavender honey, fennel seeds, and aniseed, these biscuits have a distinctive Provençal fragrance. They are the kind you'd like to always have on hand, be it with a cup of tea on the couch or on an impromptu picnic in that bright winter sun.

Mix all the dry ingredients in a bowl except the chopped almonds. Make a well in the centre and add the butter and honey. Gently mix with a fork until a ball is formed. Cover with plastic wrap and chill in the fridge for at least 30 minutes.

Pre-heat your oven to 350 °F (180 °C). Line a baking tray with parchment paper. Divide the chilled dough in 8 equal parts with a knife. Gently roll each one into a ball before putting them on the tray. Flatten them slightly, sprinkle a few fennel seeds and chopped almonds on top and bake in the oven for 15 minutes, until slightly colored on the edges.

Aniseed powder
is commonly
used in Europe for
gingerbread.
You can also find it
in Indian stores.

FOR 8 BISCUITS (3 IN./7 CM WIDE)
RESTING TIME 30 MINUTES
COOKING TIME 15 MINUTES

BANANA AND CASHEW CAKE

INGREDIENTS

3½ oz. (100 g) butter, softened

2½ oz. (70 g) muscovado sugar

2 small very ripe bananas, puréed in a blender

3½ oz. (100 g) whole rice flour, plus extra to dust

1 tsp. baking powder

a pinch of salt

2 oz. (60 g) cashews, toasted and finely ground, plus a handful roughly chopped

2 small eggs

coconut yogurt (optional), to serve

Cakes were a mainstay of my childhood. There was always one waiting for me on the counter and that's the reason I find them so reassuring. I tend to favor the rectangular shapes for practical reasons since they're easier to wrap and transport. Yes, I've been known to travel with an entire cake in my luggage, because having something sweet and familiar on hand when you're away from home is undeniably comforting. This is a nice variation on a classic banana bread. The cashews make it extra fondant, the muscovado sugar gives it a caramel-like aroma, and the rice flour keeps it light and gluten-free.

Pre-heat the oven to 350 °F (180 °C). Whisk the butter and the sugar until creamy and light. Add the puréed bananas.

In a small bowl, mix the flour, baking powder, salt, and ground cashews. Bit by bit mix the dry ingredients to the wet. Add the eggs one by one and mix to combine.

Transfer to a lightly buttered and floured cake pan, top with the chopped cashews.

Bake for 35 minutes. Let the cake cool slightly before removing it from the pan.

Serve alone or with a dollop of coconut yogurt.

Be sure to grind the cashews to a fine powder for the cake's texture to be smooth.

FOR A SMALL CAKE IN A 10 IN. (26 CM)-LONG BAKING PAN, MAKES 12 THICK SLICES
COOKING TIME 35 MINUTES

2

THE WILDER AND HARSHER SIDE OF PROVENCE, UP IN THE ROCKY MOUNTAINS, HAS A PRIMORDIAL STRENGTH TO IT.

1   Between the moss and twisted trunks, the trained eye can spot the blooming hellebores, a sign of fresh vigor in the middle of the winter.

2   A winter storm descending on the peaks. Time to find shelter below and hope the snow doesn't reach the valley.

1

AS WILDFLOWERS TURN TO FRAIL
SILHOUETTES, THE BLINDING SOLSTICE LIGHT
TURNS INTO AN ADORNMENT OF ITS OWN.

1   In the kitchen, a collection of tiny dishes that I keep reaching for. I was once told that
the smallest of tea cups were called princess cups, for it meant needing numerous refills.

2   Inside, the toned-down palette mirrors the changes in the landscape.

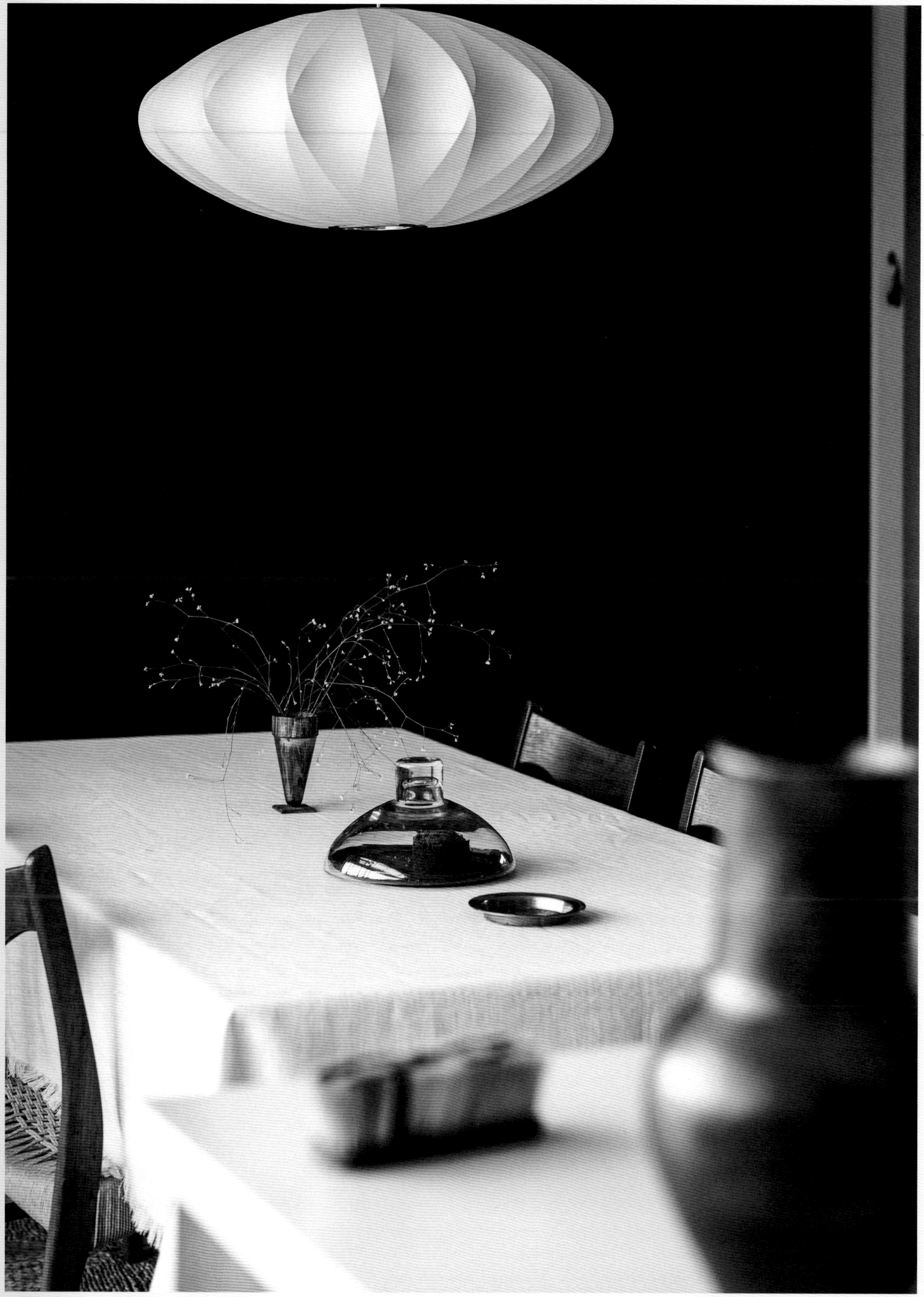

2

FOR A FEW HOURS A DAY, WINTER'S
HORIZONTAL SUN GETS WARM ENOUGH
TO OFFER THE LUXURY OF A LIGHT-
DRENCHED LUNCH ON THE TERRACE.

1   Facing the south and shielded from the mistral wind, winter gets kinder.

2   Blue-corn tortillas waiting to be filled.

INDEX

RECIPE
COLLECTIONS

ACKNOWLEDGEMENTS

A very special thank you to my husband François for getting on board in yet another adventure with me. You've braved the sun, my impatience, and my many interrogations with your legendary resilience. The cake you got in return was but a small reward for the services rendered.

Thank you to Sylvie for revealing early on the mantra to follow to complete this book on time and with a clear mind. This was priceless advice.

Thanks to Renaud and Sheri at Sigma for the photo gear.

Thank you to Andrea for believing in the project and being a benevolent presence throughout the process.

Finally, thank you to all of those who asked me if I was ever going to make a book. Each request helped turn this distant idea into the volume you're holding.

CRAFTSMEN AND SHOPS, A FEW FAVORITES

French crafts
Lola Moreau instagram.com/lolamoreau
Marion Graux Poterie à Paris instagram.com/mariongrauxpoterie
Margaux Keller margauxkeller.com
Kethevane Cellard kethevanecellard.works
Benoit Audureau instagram.com/benoit.audureau
Mano Mani manomani.fr

Japanese ceramics online
Analogue life analoguelife.com
Bows & Arrows www.japan-best.net
Toutou Kurashiki toutou-kurashiki-online-en.jp
Mayumi Yamashita etsy.com/shop/mayumiYceramics

European crafts and beyond
La Trésorerie latresorerie.fr
WholeGrainHomes wholegrainhomes.co.uk
Poloenriquez poloenriquez.com
Datcha datchaparis.com
Scarlette Ateliers scarletteateliers.com
Agustina Bottoni agustinabottoni.com

A SPOONFUL OF SUN

MEDITERRANEAN COOKBOOK
FOR ALL SEASONS

This book was conceived and edited by gestalten.

Text, photos, and illustrations by Pauline Chardin

Edited by Robert Klanten and Andrea Servert

Editorial Management by Anastasia Buryak

Design, layout, and cover: Daniel Ober, Herburg Weiland

Photo Editor: Madeleine Dudley-Yates

Typeface: GT Alpina by Reto Moser

Printed by Gutenberg Beuys Feindruckerei GmbH, Langenhagen
Made in Germany

Published by gestalten, Berlin 2022
ISBN 978-3-96704-036-4

For more information, and to order books, please visit www.gestalten.com

Bibliographic information published by the Deutsche Nationalbibliothek.
The Deutsche Nationalbibliothek lists this publication in the Deutsche Nationalbibliografie;
detailed bibliographic data is available online at www.dnb.de

This book was printed on paper certified according to the standards of the FSC®.